Summer of the Horse

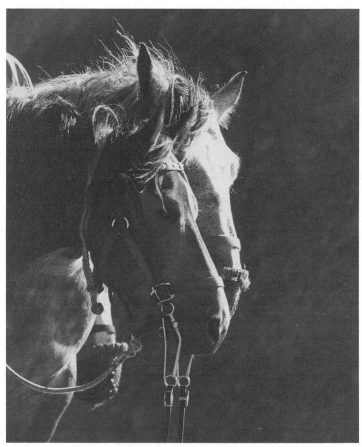

The pack string anticipates the next strenuous section of the trail.

SUMMER
of the
HORSE

Donna Kane

Lost Moose is an imprint of Harbour Publishing Co. Ltd.
P.O. Box 219, Madeira Park, BC, VON 2H0
www.harbourpublishing.com

Edited by Barbara Berson
Text design by Mary White
Map by Barbara Swail
Photos by Wayne Sawchuk unless otherwise credited
Printed in Canada

Harbour Publishing acknowledges the support of the Canada Council for the Arts, which last year invested $153 million to bring the arts to Canadians throughout the country. We also gratefully acknowledge financial support from the Government of Canada and from the Province of British Columbia through the BC Arts Council and the Book Publishing Tax Credit.

Library and Archives Canada Cataloguing in Publication

Kane, Donna, 1959–, author
     Summer of the horse / Donna Kane.
Includes bibliographical references.
Issued in print and electronic formats.
ISBN 978-1-55017-819-7 (softcover).--ISBN 978-1-55017-820-3 (HTML)
     1. Kane, Donna, 1959– —Travel--British Columbia--Muskwa-Kechika Management Area. 2. Horsemen and horsewomen—Psychology. 3. Human-animal relationships—Psychological aspects. 4. Trail riding—British Columbia—Muskwa-Kechika Management Area. 5. Packhorse camping—British Columbia--Muskwa-Kechika Management Area. 6. Muskwa-Kechika Management Area (B.C.)—Description and travel. I. Title.
SF284.4.K36 2018   636.1   C2017-906693-5
                                                                                    C2017-906694-3

for all the wild hearts

A float plane descends toward Mayfield Lakes and the next two weeks of expedition life.

Contents

ONE

Notes from the Burn

N ear the Gataga River in British Columbia's northern Rockies lies a chain of lung-shaped lakes unnamed on just about any map you look at. The most easterly lake, the one closest to the Gataga, is the one I know best because one spring I fell in love with a wilderness guide and that summer, my heart on fire, I drove up the Alaska Highway to Muncho Lake from where a float plane flew me to his cabin on the shore of what's known as Mayfield.

The first time I met Wayne I'd just flown home to northeastern BC from New York. Every chance I got, I was flying to New York. *Feature it*, as my grandmother liked to say. Feature my hooking up with a mountain man when what I thought I wanted was to live in the city.

Wayne had already arrived at his cabin with his string of horses and expedition guests after having travelled for six weeks, starting from Mile 442 of the Alaska Highway. They had crossed the Toad River into the mountains, traversed Heaven's Pass, then the Steeple and Bevin Passes, descended onto the glaciated valley of Sheep Creek, and finally crossed the Gataga to Mayfield. Accompanying me on the plane were writers, photographers, painters and filmmakers arriving for a one-week wilderness camp at Mayfield Lake. When the artist camp was over, Wayne and I would be alone for two more weeks until a final group of clients would be flown in and all of us would travel together back out to the highway. It would be Wayne's last expedition of the season and the first of its kind, ever, for me.

As our plane landed, Wayne was a speck on the wharf growing larger, the long, lean length of him taking shape as we neared: the bright coral of his dress shirt, sleeves rolled up, exposing his tanned arms; his face also tanned, a face defined by a white moustache and a square jaw and a calm and confident air, an air I did not share. I was certain I'd lose my balance walking the plane's float to the wharf, as if I were crossing from one life to another and falling would confirm my reck-lessness. As I stepped from the pontoon onto the dock, Wayne reached out his hand.

"Hi there," I said.

"You made it," Wayne said, and as we hugged, his rich laugh resonated from his chest to mine. Beside the wharf was a weathered-log sauna and beyond that a slumped-roof cabin, built on the north shore of the lake where the water was rich with swamp grass. I'd soon learn that moose liked to wade there, dunking their meteoric heads, their dewlaps sluicing the afternoon light, their rinsed bodies glistening beneath the soaring mountains, the lowering sun gilding the limestone peaks.

A few months before I'd arrived, the pine valley next to the lake had burned, the fire stopping just shy of Wayne's cabin. So all that first summer, the valley was gimped by a leafless wind. It rasped the scorched bark, crisped coals flaking off while electric-green shoots broke through the charred earth. Arnica up first, its yellow petals so immaculate it startled, then poplar and pine and willow, all in a race to begin again. The horses grazed there, swishing their tails, their ash-plumed hooves cracking open more pods, slickened seeds gummed to their silver shoes.

I was split open too, the person I'd been sloughed off, my senses a Leatherman flicking open its tools of cornea, cochlea, waft, touch, tart. Syntax glassing for anything that moved—olive-sided flycatcher, soapallalie, dwarf birch, furred muzzle of the northern caribou, sun through the thin-paned window of Wayne's cabin, its light a pale wash on the oilclothed table; a tin butter dish with enamelled roses and a blue rim; a mosquito net hung from hooks in the ceiling, draped over the bed, where our bodies, in sleep, would turn in sync. There was such relief, as if it proved some vital and necessary force had brought us together. And some kind of proof, it seemed, was what I needed.

There was a bench by the lake, its silvered planks worn smooth as the hooves of the horses grazing the burn, and we'd sit there, listening to the loons. One afternoon a family of otters swam near the shore, formed a circle and played, and I felt so far from home, sick with guilt for having left my husband, and aching for my children, though they were grown. There were days when, overcome with what I'd done, I'd leap from the wharf just to feel water's axe-smack stripping off thought like a seed head slipped from its saw-toothed stalk—awareness deboned of thought, a gawking shimmering socket.

We rode the horses on a trail up to the alpine, where the air was thin as a marmot's whistle; where frost boiled up through glacial till, split plates of shale into toothy sprockets; where caribou tracks pestled the scree and moss campion grew in the hollows of their steps. When I walked on the caribou lichen (*Cladonia rangiferina*), it crunched like cornflakes. I felt first like a giant whose ill-placed steps were crushing a coral floor, then Lilliputian, sitting on the ridge, staring at mountains racked peak after peak. So much space and so much silence. Below, I could see Mayfield Lake, where Wayne had asked, "Do you think you could live here?"

Every sound seemed directed at me, every gust of wind, every bunting darting by—muscles on a pull-string—every squirrel ratcheting in the trees, spruce needles clattering to the ground, the horse bells tolling. This was the news I received.

One day I walked into the burn and found an insect that looked like the charred forest incarnate, its body black as charcoal, witching the root of a burned-out tree with its brittle antennae, its legs the rusty orange of dead spruce needles, its wings rattling and sizzling, a new exuberance rising from the wreckage. For a moment I could delete the past. I walked back to the cabin and stood there, my hand on the small of Wayne's back, beside a lake whose mud bottom was etched with beaver trails, its surface whisked by merganser wings. Where the water was shallow and fleshy with grass and moose plunged their heads, I gathered up my love and moved forward.

Wayne Sawchuk has led expeditions through the Muskwa–Kechika for over thirty years. SALLY PULESTON MCINTOSH

TWO

Book Fair

I used to live in a big white farmhouse in the crook of a valley next to my parents' farm. My husband and I built the house. It had a covered porch, a veranda that faced west, where on summer evenings we would sit with our two children and look toward the horizon, past my father's fields, the warm air filled with the sweet smell of cut hay, the chaff from the mower pinked by the sun setting behind the foothills of the Rocky Mountains.

The foothills were a haze of blue in the distance, a velvet backdrop to our busy lives. I couldn't have imagined then that I would one day wake inside a tent pitched beside a river many passes north of that mountain range and that the person beside me would be another man.

When I tell people that I met Wayne at the Dawson Creek Municipal Public Library at a local authors' book fair, their response is often bemusement, the setting so benign. I remember thinking I didn't want to go to the book fair. I had just returned from a trip to New York with friends. I was wearing a purple blouse I'd bought at Macy's and a black skirt, and my shoes had also been bought in New York in a little boutique off Fifth Avenue. My friend Ruth had talked me into them. On the day of the book fair, under all the bristle of my recent trip was a dead eros. I was forty-seven. My husband and I, married for twenty-five years, spent our evenings in different rooms—he in the living room reading and me in my study writing. Our two children were grown. For a long time we'd been saying that we needed to find more in common, but a kind of inertia had taken hold.

I was late, and I rushed in and there, seated at their tables, were retired teachers eager to show what they'd published and a man with his personal memoir of moving to the Peace Country. Before I saw Wayne I saw his book, a coffee table–sized hardcover with a photo of a moose on its glossy cover, propped up on a display stand. I had heard about the book, and I knew the name of the author. My best friend, Emilie, and I had talked about Wayne's photographs of the Muskwa–Kechika, a wilderness area in BC's northern Rockies. To have taken such photos seemed exotic to me, and despite Wayne's Ukrainian last name, he seemed a natural part of that wild world he now helped to protect.

The tables at the library were arranged in the shape of a horseshoe, with everyone sitting on the outside looking into the centre. Wayne's table was on one side of the U and I saw my place name set on a table on the other side—directly opposite, so that, sitting in our respective spots, we'd be facing each other from across the room. I stood in the centre, my back to Wayne, arranging my table display of one thin volume of poetry and several copies of an issue of *BC Bookworld* that included a short review of my book. Feeling the presence of someone behind me, I turned around. He looked a bit older than in the photographs I'd seen, but I recognized him. "You must be Wayne Sawchuk."

"And you're Donna Kane."

His handshake matched mine. As I remember it now, at that moment we lit up, standing together inside the U, having an introductory chat that went on for quite a while, soon becoming banter and possibly flirtation. When I look back on it, I think of those other authors, Betty and Walter and the rest of them, how they witnessed a moment of chance that would set off an impassioned fuse of destruction—the instant in which our lives changed. Was it visible?

I bought a copy of Wayne's book. He bought a copy of mine. He offered to show me some photos from his summer expedition in the Rockies. We knew nothing about each other, but we both felt compelled to follow up with a ridiculous flurry of emails. He sent the first one. Why is this still so important to me?

Before I told my husband and before Wayne told his partner, Wayne came to me and got down on his knees and said, "You're the first woman I've said I loved and really meant it." The speed of our coming together meant we had no song, no symbols or objects that would serve as reminders of first dates or anniversaries of when we met. After that first handshake, the rest became a blur, our bodies moving while our minds raced to keep up.

THREE

First Summer on the Trail

Wayne is dressed and out of the tent before I've managed to open my eyes. One of the guests has already lit the campfire and set a kettle of water on the grill. Others are rummaging through panniers asking for the oatmeal, and a delighted voice cries out, "Oh look, here it is!"

It's six in the morning. How can they be so chipper? As Wayne walks toward the group, I listen for his greeting, each morning the same, filled with the kind of cheer that inspires optimism, the words lifting then falling—"Good morning, good morning."

It's not easy for me to jump into these early conversations, so I stay inside to pack up our sleeping bags and air mattresses while Wayne helps with breakfast and brings me a cup of strong coffee.

During one of these breakfast chats, I hear

one of the guests tell Wayne he's been married forty-two years.

"These days," the man says, "when people vow, 'till death do us part,' what they really mean is, 'until we get bored.'"

Was that what happened with my twenty-five-year marriage? I press my knees into the mattress, focusing hard on the wheeze of expelled air.

By the time I have taken down the tent, eaten my oatmeal and washed the Melmac dishes in a plastic tub, Wayne has collected the halters and is ready to find the horses.

We hike off together, leaving the rest of the crew—Michael, a retired bureaucrat, his friend and former colleague Liz, who works to protect the burrowing owl, and Shirley, a young student from Montreal—to put away the cooking gear and wrap sleeping bags and tents inside canvas tarps, turning them into soft packs for the horses to carry.

At the start of my twenty-five-year marriage, I took my husband's last name. When the marriage ended, I went to the government office and filled out the form to get my birth name back: Donna Haight. With the ink still fresh from my reclaimed signature, I walked back to my car. I felt light-headed. I drove to the house I now shared with Wayne, pulled into the driveway and shut off the engine. I sat there, taking a moment to let it sink in. I picked up the yellow form from the passenger seat, unfolded it and stared hard at my signature. My handwriting had changed so much since the last time I'd written my birth name. Maybe it was the calligraphy classes I'd taken, something I'd done before my kids were in school, before I'd gone back to college, before I studied visual arts, before I turned to writing. I looked again at my signature. Who was Donna Haight?

I had been Donna Kane for more years than I had been that other woman. "Donna Kane!" Emilie's granddaughter said, whenever she saw me. "Donna Kane," the receptionist said, when I arrived at work. Over time, my first and last name had become one, the two words seeming to fit together in rhythm and sound. For me, hearing my full name spoken made me feel more solidly a part of the world. Hearing my full name spoken gave me comfort. Donna *Haight* was someone I no longer knew.

I started the car and returned to the government office and asked to have my name changed back to Kane. The woman who had helped before was still behind the counter. She must have seen it all. She shrugged and gave a little smile. "Not a problem," she said. "No big deal."

I may have left a major part of my life behind, but the experiences of that past will continue to be a part of who I am.

My halter slung over my shoulder, I follow Wayne. The horses are herd-bound, so haltering a few of the lead horses is usually enough to convince the rest to follow us back to camp. This year there are seventeen in all: seven for riding, nine for packing, and a spare, in case a horse is injured and needs a day off. Bringing them back to camp can be exciting if the horses are far away and you have to ride your horse bareback. Their hobbles, loops of rope tied around their forelegs to slow their travel in the night, are now removed, leaving the horses fancy-free, frisky from a night of rest and food and working each other into a frenzy as they tussle for a position in line.

For three months of the year, this is the horses' life. Each day they carry their riders or soft packs or bright orange panniers filled with tins of fish and bags of rice over the mountain passes of the northern Rockies, descending into boreal forest, along swamps and sand flats, across creeks and rivers, to finally arrive at camp, where they are unpacked, hobbled and let go for the night. In the morning, we find them where the grass suits them best or where Hazel, the alpha of the herd, has had a mind to go. For three months of each year, it is Wayne's life too.

Some of the people who join Wayne on his expeditions are already familiar with the outdoors, while others have never experienced wilderness and this is their chance. Some want to become more aware of the Muskwa–Kechika, others are simply curious to see what it will be like, for them, to be in wilderness. It's not advertised as such, but many of the people who sign up for Wayne's expeditions are looking for something. Adventure, sure, but many come to reflect on where their life is at, or, more precisely, to have second thoughts about where their life is at. Being in a place disconnected from any communication with the regular world, standing on the top of a mountain pass, looking as far as you can and seeing no sign of human intervention, clears your head, shows you what's important. Tells you what's not. Last summer, one of the folks came off the trail, went home, quit his job, left his girlfriend, and last I heard he'd moved into a cabin north of Pemberton.

Every two weeks a new group comes in to replace those going out, a rotation that continues throughout the summer. They arrive by float plane, landing on a nearby lake, or they come in on a small-wheeled plane that sets them down on an airstrip belonging to an outfitter's camp—a camp that might include a makeshift corral from logs once peeled, now furred by moss and lichen, a few buildings with elk antlers over the door lintels and, if a building is made of plywood, a wall bashed in where a grizzly has walked through as if it were cardboard, having caught a whiff of dried moose blood or someone's forgotten cheese sandwich.

Before Wayne became a conservationist, before he was guiding eco-tourists through the mountains, he was a logger and a hunting guide. As we hike along in our search for the horses, Wayne stops to peer into a small dip in the trail filled with rain from a recent storm.

"What is it?" I ask.

"Wolf," he says, pointing at the paw print, the track appearing magnified through the water.

We look along the trail for other tracks, for the prints of the horses' hooves, which will tell us the speed and direction of travel. The signs of movement, of change, are everywhere. It's how we recognize life. Wayne stops. I stop. Both of us listen for the horses' bells. I think I hear them, but I'm too unsure to say so. Maybe what I hear is a bird. Maybe it's the clinking of the halter's buckle against my shoulder. "There they are," Wayne says.

The first time Wayne introduced me to the horses, I spooked them. I moved too quickly, I waved my hands in front of their faces. They could sense my nervousness and became nervous too. Although I've come to know them better and have now learned the different dispositions and personalities of each, I still seem to end up putting things on backwards or in the wrong order. Things such as halters. More than once Hazel has tried to shove her nose past my hands as they fumble with what feels like a Gordian knot, as if trying to help or say, *Okay. Just stop. I'll show you how it's done, and pay attention so you get it right the next time.*

I rehearse the steps in my mind as I walk: Approach a horse from its left side and stay calm. Use your left hand to orient the halter, your right to bring the crown strap over the horse's large head. I think of Sunny the Belgian—I am sure that if I curled into a fetal position, I could fit inside her skull.

I walk up to Hazel. Once the halter is on, I have to do up the buckle. Seeing a buckle on a halter and being unable to cinch it up is to see a buckle in a whole new way. How had I failed to notice the tang, like a miniature crowbar with a tapered tip, how it rests in that small groove etched in the right-hand side of the buckle's rim, the tang's other end bent around the cross brace that splits the frame in two? How did

I not see that the two windows formed by the middle brace are not the same size, the opening between the crossbar and the groove the exact reach for the tang, while the other side is wider, so that the tang, when flicked across that gap, can't reach the far edge.

I have twisted the crown strap of the halter, the buckle flipped upside down so that the wider side of the buckle's frame is closest to the tang. Realizing this makes all the difference when I've spent too much time situating the halter and the buckle won't buckle and now all the other horses are unhobbled and heading with gusto back to camp. I feed the strap through the larger window. The tang can't catch and I am bewildered, struck by wildness, what I am left with when everything I know has changed.

It was fall when, for the last time, I left the house I'd lived in, the house where my children had grown up, making their way from kindergarten to university; a home where Christmas decorations were made from playdough one year, clothespins the next, where stories were read one chapter a night, unless the hobbit was in serious danger, then we'd read more, where habits were so comfortable and deep you didn't even know they were there.

The house having sold, I'd gone back to wash the floors, the cupboards, to pack up the last of my belongings, and to spend one last night in the house with my daughter. She'd come home from university for the summer to be with her father, the man who had been my husband for twenty-five years, a good husband, but now, somehow, not good enough. On my last night there he was working night shift, his work schedule still something I know off by heart.

The next morning the sun shone through the lilac leaves whose bushes I'd dug from my grandmother's garden and transplanted beneath the kitchen window. The shrubs grown so large they required regular trimming to keep them from blocking sunlight through the windowpane—light that had touched our faces as we made toast, poured coffee, made plans for the day. The red-winged blackbirds sang by the pond (scolded, really), my daughter still asleep in her room (no, not asleep; she was still in bed, but we had said goodbye, her face firm and resolute, insisting, as she always has, "I'm fine."). Outside, I looked up at her window, where she wasn't sleeping. I looked at the pond, at the trees, at the copper lanterns, with their candles inside, hanging from the eaves of the covered porch. Each look a leave-taking.

We return with the horses to camp, me leading Hazel, who is anxious because we have lagged behind. Once in camp, the horses are saddled and packed, and our day on the trail begins. Wayne's horse, Bonus, is spirited and moves faster at a walk than most of the other horses in trot. Bonus tosses his dark mane, his taut neck muscles giving him a regal air as Wayne, his body lean and strong, holds him back as best he can, the rest of the string falling behind regardless. When the distance is such that the other horses are whinnying madly, or a guest at the back is calling to the front, Wayne waits for us to catch up. Usually, by the time we've closed the gap, Wayne has already slipped his camera or binoculars back into his saddlebag, and all we see is his backside fielding a trot with an air of yippee-ki-yay.

But this morning, at the foot of a pass, Wayne stops long enough to show me a dip at the edge of a bank. Where the meadow was exposed to the spring's full sun, cow parsnip, hellebore, lupines and asters shot up, bloomed and flourished through the summer, and now, with September in hand, their stalks have turned to straw, the flowers fisted into seed. Without a measurable distance between them, the shaded flowers, where the snow was late to melt, are still glossy with an off-kilter spring, their leaves plump with chlorophyll, stamens dusting their brittle neighbours with pollen. Both patches had the same potential to bloom, to make seed, but it was external conditions, the sun with its light and heat, that determined when that potential would be realized.

"Choice, what choice?" Wayne will say when I go over, again, our choice to make a life together. The first time I heard him say it, it seemed at odds with his pragmatic nature, but I don't think he was being romantic. Or, if he was, then it was a romance defined as a belief in the necessity to recognize one's potential. We responded to each other not because we were unaware of the havoc our actions would cause, but because choice, as Wayne said, was not part of the equation.

But was that really so for me? I might not have had a choice over the resonance I felt, or how that resonance would come, but I could have resisted it. Like the plants at the foot of Bevin Pass, I am compelled by the external world, forces that bring me to yes. To no. For me, there is also *maybe*. I chose to leave my old life behind. *You were bored*, a voice says, *you wanted an adventure*. Yes. No. Maybe there will never be an answer good enough.

FOUR

Where He Comes From

Wayne's mother must have loved wild men. Although she was kind and gentle and refused to learn how to use a rifle, she allowed her sons to aim theirs out the kitchen window to take potshots at squirrels and birds. Her husband, Mike, smashed dishes when in a rage. Once, Freda surprised them all by smashing a dish too, then another, until there were no dishes left, at which point, or so the story goes, she threw the kitchen chair out the front door. The chair lay on its side until it yellowed the grass beneath it and the veneer began to blister from the rain and dew. It was Mike who brought the chair back in.

Wayne grew up near Hasler Flats, just west of Chetwynd in northeastern BC, with his parents, two brothers and a sister. Their home was set in a forest of spruce and aspen along the Pine River. His grandparents lived on the Pine too, a few miles downstream.

Southeast of both homes, the Sukunka River enters the Pine after arcing around a foothill that forms part of the eastern slopes of the Rocky Mountains. When Wayne was fourteen, he figured if he could hitch a ride to the Sukunka side of the foothill, ahead of where it joined the Pine, cross the river and then hike over the hill, heading slightly northwest, he'd end up back at his grandmother's house. She made excellent biscuits and stew. If anyone asked, he would say he wanted to walk from one river to the other for the adventure of it. Maybe he wanted to impress his grandmother. But I think it also had to do with the fact that the two rivers converged, that the Sukunka disappeared into the Pine. Wayne loves to tell how rivers slice through rocks as if mountains were cheese, and that many of the rivers in the north were flowing before the mountains were formed.

By the time Wayne was fourteen, he was reading everything he could about geology, about the age of rocks and the way they layer and how they grind themselves down. He liked the idea of seeing the present becoming the past. To the southeast of Chetwynd, the Sukunka is in the present; a few miles north, downstream, it is in the past.

No one else wanted to go with him, so Wayne had his parents drive him to the south side of the foothill and leave him on the bank of the river. After watching the dust billowing behind the tail lights of their blue Volkswagen Beetle, he started to undress.

With his boots, socks, jeans and briefs tied to his Trapper Nelson packboard, he made his way across the Sukunka River. In his pack he also carried an axe, matches, a plastic tarp and a sleeping bag. Also three cans of Irish stew and a package of red Twizzlers, a 30-30 calibre rifle with shells, and a hunting knife. It was early September.

If his father worried about Wayne, he never showed it. That summer Mike had shot a bear in the back, wounding but not killing it. He brought his emptied rifle to Wayne and told him to finish the job, gesturing impatiently in the general direction of where he'd shot the bear. "I gotta go to work," he said, and went off in a huff. You could say he was trying to teach Wayne how to survive, and that would be true.

The canvas-and-wood pack was heavy and the cans of stew threatened to throw Wayne off balance as his bare feet slipped over the stones on the river bottom. He knew how to ford a river, recognizing where to cross by the ripples that chopped the water, but the Sukunka still rose to his chest and its northern cold numbed him from the heart down. When he reached the other side, he felt alive and triumphant. His body invigorated, he wobbled about on the stones along the beach, careful to keep dirt out of his socks. He saw the track of a black bear incised in the sand, the print clear and sharp, the fine lines that mapped its calloused pad, the press of each toe. He could even make out the small flame of one claw.

The trip to his grandmother's house couldn't be made in one day, and that was part of the plan. A few yards from a small pond where the clay was rich with minerals, creating a natural lick for wildlife, he set up camp, tying a sheet of plastic between two trees with some rope. He had read many books on knots, and his fingers looped the rope into bowlines with ease. He found two aspen logs and placed them on the ground, parallel to each other. Gathering bits of twigs woolly with witch's hair lichen from under a spruce tree's spreading branches, he made a small pile. With his hands cupped around a match, he struck and lit the kindling in one go. He was pleased. He added bigger twigs, and then branches of aspen and willow. Standing over the fire, Wayne was a young man glowing with the energy of independence. Like the flames, he was blazing on his own.

He ate a can of stew. He thought of the girl in his math class who bought records by the Bay City Rollers and wore a tartan vest. Like many of his friends, Wayne had been growing his hair longer. His father hated it. He heard a splash and saw a cow moose in the pond, close to the edge, licking the mineral-rich clay along the shore. Wayne gripped his rifle and watched. It grew dark, but the moose stayed put. When she did leave, Wayne could no longer make out her form in the night, but as she went he heard her hooves crunch the crisp poplar leaves on the ground, one hoof knocking a wind-fallen log.

Wayne stoked the fire for several hours. He felt himself suspended in a bubble of light in the midst of a vast, dark universe that went on forever. He was aware of being inside his particular body, his particular bones. Although his parents were Seventh-day Adventists, Wayne no longer believed in God. For him, no one else was on this side of the river. He was alone. He heard a twig crack. Then silence. Something, maybe the wind, maybe a mouse, rustled some leaves. He listened so intently that he could track the sound of the wind, hearing it first as a rolling wave, a surf surging between the trunks of the trees and then the clatter of leaves. He heard another splash, and then the quacking of ducks. Finally he let the fire burn down and, curling up in his sleeping bag, he tugged the drawstring tight around his face.

He was up early. He liked that he was *breaking camp*, a phrase he had read in books about explorers. He had read everything he could find about wild places. *Three Against the Wilderness* was his current favourite, a story of homesteading in BC's Chilcotins. It seemed to him that the people in the story led exotic lives on a wild and perilous frontier. It didn't occur to him that his life on the Pine River was equally wild, giving him the skills he would need to live in the wilderness himself. He didn't realize that the wilderness had been pushed north year by year, that the Chilcotins were no longer the frontier, that the frontier was all around him. He walked down to the lick and saw fresh tracks of moose, of deer and elk—a life going on. In the night he had not been alone; he'd been a part of that life; he'd been their neighbour.

Wayne shouldered his pack and struck through the heavy forest where aspen windfall slowed him down and thorns from the rose bushes caught on his jeans. Then the sloping hill rose sharply, the aspens growing smaller and the grassy slopes giving way to a band of grey sandstone. Looking for a way around the cliff face would have seemed a failure to him, so he climbed higher on the rock, his rifle in one hand, an axe in the other. He reached a broad horizontal ledge that led to the left and around a corner. Above him, the face of the rock bulged outward. The ledge grew narrower but there was something at the heart of this boy that knew only forward. The rubber soles of his hiking boots gripped the edge of the ridge but then slipped on a loose piece of rock and his pack swung sideways. He fell. Nothing in the moment of his falling seemed in any way a part of him. He landed on his back, hard, head facing downhill. He felt the weight of his pack slam into his shoulders before he slid down the scree, through bramble bushes, his body coming to rest against the trunk of a small aspen. His axe had left a deep gash in the stock of his rifle but his bones were unscathed. At first, he was stunned by his fallibility. Then he was amazed by his intactness, a kind of shock that helped him realize he was a part of the mortal world.

He paused, ate a Twizzler and considered a safer route. It took him a few hours to climb a grassy slope that brought him to a crest. He began to work his way along the slope of pine and aspen, the forest thickening with alder and willow and then small bogs with black spruce that he had to pick his way through carefully, so as not to get sucked into the mire. Now he had to use his navigation skills, finding markers as guideposts.

As he made his way through the thick bush, over moss and past shrubs of Labrador tea, he watched the sun and made sure he kept it at a constant angle.

The mountain sloped gently downward now, and finally, occasionally, he could catch a glimpse of the deep valley of the Pine. He felt a sense of comfort as well as disappointment that his adventure was coming to a close. He reached a rough road that descended to the riverbank. He would cross the river and then he would make his way past the beach and up onto the highway that led to the driveway of his grandmother's house. He looked back at where he had come from; he looked ahead. He knew where he was and where he was going.

Chrissie gets braver with members of the expedition.

FIVE

Ulla

Ulla, one of Wayne's pack horses, had given birth to a foal in the spring. All during our first summer together, Wayne worked to gain Chrissie's trust. As I watched him spend time with the young horse, quietly walking around her, standing close but not interfering, I could see my own shyness reflected in Chrissie's. I could see how both of us were becoming more used to the trail. Parts of me were growing calmer too, less worried about riding Hazel, my confidence building to where I might click my tongue for Hazel to go and mean it. And tasks like setting up tent poles or putting a bit into a horse's mouth caused me less fluster than they had at first.

If I managed to get my riding horse saddled and bridled and ready to go in time to help with the pack horses, it was always Ulla's gear I went for. Ulla didn't spook easily. I'd scan the horse crowd looking for a heavy-set dark bay. She'd stand quietly, tolerant of me even if I put the pack saddle on backwards or if I forgot that the blanket goes over the pad and I needed to take the whole thing off and start again. Ulla was unflappable, but also indifferent. She wasn't a horse who vied for human attention. And I was okay with that, my feelings leaning more toward gratitude than kinship.

While Ulla went about her quiet way, her nimble grey foal, Chrissie, would run up and down the pack line, playful and spirited by curiosity. When we stopped on the trail for lunch, Chrissie would come over to sniff our waxed cheeses and tins of fish. If she was feeling extra brave, she might nibble the brim of my hat. By late August, Wayne was able to place his hand on Chrissie's neck, to stroke her back and feed her alfalfa pellets out of his hand.

Autumn was not far off. It was, in fact, making a bigger presence each day. The leaves of the buckbrush, the poplar, the Labrador tea, had started to shut off their chlorophyll, closing up shop. The bearberry plant was so red it seemed lit from within. The speckles of brown on the orange and red leaves of the dwarf birch were like chips of blown glass in the afternoon sun.

During a rest day at Bevin Lake, a kilometre west of the Rocky Mountain divide, Wayne decided to put a halter on Chrissie. He rummaged through the orange panniers and unearthed a small, yellow headstall from beneath the horse bells and nose baskets, chunks of leather and rope. To put the halter on Chrissie meant bringing the whole pack string into camp. Herdbound, all horses move as one.

The horses were spending their rest day grazing on the hills that sloped into Bevin Lake. We were camped a short distance away, beside a creek that had startled me when we'd first arrived, the water a deep turquoise, the boulders it tumbled over coated white by a mineral that seeped from the rock glacier above. The creek looked Caribbean, as if I might see a cabana along the shore attended by someone in flowery shorts selling margaritas.

When we reached the lake, the water's translucent green reflected the puffs of cumulus clouds, the surrounding landscape and the horses. Most had their necks bent down, their noses in the grass. I admired the way they scanned the plants with their velvety muzzles, their lips brushing each stalk and blossom, sensing by smell or perhaps by feel the difference in texture and weight between the lupines, which they liked, and the cow parsnip, which they did not, selecting goose grass and bluebells with the speed and dexterity of rummage sale shoppers.

When we reached the herd, we removed their hobbles. The first time I had watched a horse being restrained in this way, I was appalled. With the horse's front legs bound a few inches apart, the hobbles looked like a medieval torture device. Wayne uses a twist hobble, a length of soft rope that is tied around a front leg then twisted around itself (three times is best) before being tied to the other leg. It seemed hard to imagine how a horse would be comfortable in such a contraption, let alone able to move. But a hobbled horse can travel up a mountain pass and down the other side in a single night while the humans are sleeping. If a moose ambles into the fray, a horse can forgo its leisurely gunny-sack hop and bound like a rabbit with impressive speed.

We freed the horses of their legholds, then haltered a few to lead back to camp, knowing the rest would follow. Once at camp, we kept the horses tied up while Wayne made a makeshift corral by stringing a length of rope around a circle of trees. He led Ulla inside the circle and Chrissie followed. Chrissie wasn't convinced that a halter was anything she wanted or needed, but eventually Wayne was able to slip it on her. I video-taped the event, and when we watched it later, we could see Chrissie, skittish and wary, while Ulla stood quietly to the side, seemingly undisturbed.

With Chrissie sporting her new halter, we untied the rest of the horses and put their hobbles back on. Hobbles are synonymous with eating, so the horses are eager to be back in them. Ulla, however, kicked at her stomach and began to roll. It was unusual for a horse not to follow the others. While horses will often roll after a day's work, rubbing away the salt and sweat from the weight of their packs, on that day Ulla's behaviour was different. Wayne removed her hobbles so she could move around more easily, then watched in his calm yet considered way as she dawdled and fretted.

Wayne carries a few veterinary supplies—salve for cuts or sores, a tube of bute in case a horse is in pain—but a horse who requires a vet is out of luck. A hundred miles from the nearest road, at the foot of the Rocky Mountain divide where water splits in two, flows east and west, near a lake too small for a float plane to land, there is no easy way out.

By evening Ulla and Chrissie had moved closer to the other horses, and though Ulla still seemed uncomfortable, she didn't seem worse. We hoped that whatever was bothering her would pass like a bad case of heartburn. Perhaps a bit of larkspur, a plant thought to be poisonous to horses, had been wrapped up with a lupine and she'd swallowed it in haste. Our group was quieter that evening, everyone retreating to their tents early, as if that might make the morning, and with it a recovered Ulla, come more quickly.

When Chrissie whinnied into camp, her voice entered my sleep the way frost feathers a pane of glass. A shiver pinpricking its way into whatever dream I was having inside a tent that blocked the light from the moon and stars. In those first few minutes of waking, it was so dark that I couldn't make out the shape of my body. I couldn't make out the shape of Wayne's. Chrissie whinnied again, and this time my stomach gave a little flip.

Wayne groped for his headlamp, turned it on and looked at his watch—3:00 a.m. He pulled on his pants and shirt and unzipped the tent door.

"Should I come with you?" I asked.

"No, I'll check things out and let you know."

I was relieved. It was cold. I was tired. I still felt useless when it came to the horses.

I could hear Wayne talking to Chrissie in his calm, reassuring voice: "Hey Chrissie, how are you doing? Where's your Mom? I don't see your Mom."

As his footsteps faded from camp, I pulled the sleeping bag tight. The warmth from Wayne's body was quickly dissipating in the chilled air. I lay with my sleeping bag drawn tight around me, Wayne and Chrissie invisible weights in the night. I fell back into a light sleep but woke when I heard Wayne's footsteps returning to the tent. He slipped back inside.

"No sign of Ulla. We'll have to wait until morning."

We lay beside each other with only the sound of the creek rushing by.

"It's a beautiful night," Wayne said. "The stars are glittering away."

In the morning a skim of ice had formed in the water pail. The sky was clear, the air bright and crisp. After coffee and oatmeal, Wayne began to sort through the bridles, getting ready to find the horses and to look for Ulla. For most of the past two weeks, it had been me or Michael, a seasoned guest who returned each year to spend time on the trail, who accompanied Wayne on these morning treks, the rest of the group staying behind to pack up. But that morning, everyone wanted to go. Including me. It was like knowing there was a traffic accident ahead. Instead of avoiding the crash site, everyone wanted to change their course to ensure they'd pass by. But with every guest determined to go, I offered to stay and pack up. Armed with cameras and bridles, the group headed off. Maybe Ulla had caught her leg between some rocks or was in some other form of distress and every hand would be needed. Chrissie had left Ulla in the night and returned to our camp. If Chrissie was no longer in Ulla's care, it followed that Ulla must have been unable to care for Chrissie.

I washed the dishes, put the grills and pots in their respective storage bags, packed them into the panniers, made lunch for the trail, took down the tent and doused the fire, retrieving bits of unburned material. Close to being finished, it occurred to me that if Ulla were alive but in need of convalescence, everything I'd packed up would have to be undone. Resentment took hold, not of the trail but of what it took to be on the trail. And maybe not even what it took to be on the trail, but at how inept I was. Wayne had moved through each task for so many years he no longer thought about it, but for me, everything was a struggle. There was a precise order to the way each chore was done. While I understood the necessity for this—how the many moving parts of a pack string needed to stay intact, that it was part of what ensured our overall safety—it irked me. Had I, in some crazy twist of fate, ended a quarter-century marriage for a relationship in which I had less autonomy than before?

Nothing in my past life seemed to serve me here. Never would I have signed up for such a trip in my former life. I was comfortable in the outdoors, but hiking along the river didn't require the same set of skills needed to be part of a pack string. And it seemed to me that everyone who came on the trail was maddeningly confident, believing in themselves in a way I did not, carrying out each task in a state of perpetual good cheer. I could see how they loved not just the wilderness but their bodies in it. There was a healthy pride in their abilities, one that didn't make them defensive or churlish when they did something wrong. How happy they were, recounting their adventures around the fire at night or bent down at Wayne's tent, offering him a cup of coffee, saying that if only they didn't have to return to their jobs they would stay on the trail forever.

As I marched around the camp I thought, *It would be easier if Ulla were dead.* The thought was terrible and selfish, but for an instant it came, and then it was gone.

When the group returned, I could see Wayne in the lead, riding Bonus. He had a grim look on his face.

"Ulla's dead."

I listened, camp flunky, overseer of the Melmac cups, as everyone described Ulla, gibbous in the lake. She must have walked into the water for relief, Wayne said, and then drowned. She was found floating on her side, coasting on her reflection. An equine Ophelia, her mane fanning out on the water, the sun silvering her hair. I should have seen it, they kept telling me: it was tragic, but strangely beautiful. They seemed to bristle with the tragedy but also with the privilege of having witnessed something new. I stared at Wayne, busy packing up the horses, moving forward. Something in his being kept him from getting emotional.

"Didn't it bother you?" I asked him some days later.

"Of course, but you can't let emotions steer the ship. Your survival depends on having a practical response. What I thought was, *Well, it's a sad thing, now we have a foal to deal with, what's going to happen to her, who's going to take Ulla's saddle.* There were practical issues to deal with, a limited set of options, and emotions aren't one of them. If a moose charges you," Wayne continued, "screaming isn't going to help. You'd better find the nearest tree."

We packed up the horses and headed up Bevin Pass. As we led them up the scree, a thick chamber of cloud filled the valley below. Like whipped cream being piped from an icing gun, a venturi effect formed where the moist and constricted air of the valley met the colder winds sweeping down the hill. A seraph, a tribute, and beyond it we could now see the lake, though Ulla was too small to make out.

"My good horse Ulla," Wayne said, as we looked down at the speck of blue. "It wasn't common, the way the wind coasted her around the lake. It was so out of context for a horse."

I thought of how out of context I had been all summer, how difficult it had been to connect with my surroundings, to embrace the horses, to feel I fit in with the other guests. It had made me self-absorbed. I felt a pang of shame.

Chrissie followed the other horses and their riders up the pass, Wayne in the lead. How quickly Chrissie stopped whinnying, her mind focused now on not being left behind. Had she watched Ulla floating on the lake as if she were nothing but a dewdrop on a lupine leaf? I thought of Ulla, how the wind would eventually drift her to shore. No longer Chrissie's mom, she would become carrion to ravens, bears and wolves. She would bloat. Finally, she would be nothing but bone. The nails in her horseshoes would loosen and the shoes would slip from her shrunken hooves; if the hooves were still in the water, the horseshoes might clink together as they sank, silver and U-shaped, flipping end over end as they fell to the bottom.

Ulla had been, the others kept repeating, something to see, her body luminescent, bathed as she was in an otherworldly light.

SIX

Tracks

At the top of Bevin Pass, all of us—the dog, the horses and the riders who have led the horses up the sharp incline—stop to catch our breath. I am sweating from the exertion of the climb and from the heat of the morning sun burning through the alpine air, but my bones still throb from the keen wind of the valley floor now two thousand feet below. Like a Baked Alaska, those fancy ice cream desserts that are oven-cooked, my body is simultaneously engaged in two very different temperatures, the cold from the past and the heat from the present.

I listen to my breath expending itself on a mountain pass—breath from the same body still chilled from the valley; breath from the same body that once moved through the Peace River farmland where I grew up and raised my children, a place where I'd walk through a grove of poplar and willow trees along a path that led to my parents' yard, testing the season through the timothy that grew along the trail. In spring, I would pull on the stalks and they would unsleeve, thin pipings whose ends would be dark and flush with sap, sweet in my mouth. By fall, I'd pull on the stalks and the once green, dense heads would have bleached and dried. For an instant, before dissembling into a heap of minuscule seeds, the timothy head would keep its shape in my hand. It always seemed that in that moment, when the seed head was pulled from the stalk but stayed whole, I'd come as close to experiencing a liminal state as I ever had, a threshold between past and present. On the scree slope trail of rock debris, I feel the same enlivening sense that in a single moment I can discern two distinct experiences.

I've always felt a need to know that threshold, the still point, the seam, the defining thing that holds each change together. As if there were some omniscience to it. Maybe if I experienced that fulcrum, that moment distinct from the things on either side of change, I might know everything there is to know.

On a scree slope, it is not really possible to identify individual tracks. Standing at the top of the pass I look behind me and see a shadow leading up to where I am, a line that continues over the other side, a trail formed by a composite weathering of shale weighed down by the travels of caribou, sheep, bears, and now our group of horses and humans, each in their turn crushing bits of rock, pressing them a little more solidly into the earth. Shadows pool inside the subtle hollow formed from this packing down and that is the track I see—not the individual steps, but an overall movement.

When I think of my own movements, the progression of events that have brought me from birth to the top of this mountain pass, when I try to delineate the different experiences that have propelled me, I can't. Everything, from the Charlie McCarthy ventriloquist doll that frightened me as a child, to watching my grandma turn strawberries into jam, to swimming in the silty waters of the Kiskatinaw River, listening to Ella Fitzgerald, falling in love, then out of love, watching my son and my daughter grow up and leave home, all bind together into who I am. I can remember individual events. I can say things like, "It was in that moment that Wayne and I shook hands," but the things that built into that moment of realization are impossible to separate. Maybe, like the shadow that pools in this alpine trail, I have a shadow too. Maybe that's what awareness is, a shadow that emerges from all my impressions.

Time is another word for drift, for the seamless motion of one thing turning into the next, a stiffening stalk, a subtle shift in colour. To be alive is to be in motion, a constant state of change.

At the crest of Bevin Pass, where the view of the valleys and distant mountain ranges is most exposed, just a few feet off the trail, a collection of stones are arranged in two parallel lines on the ground, the space between just wide enough for a human body to lie horizontally. Tufts of alpine grass and a silting in of dirt have built up around the base of the rocks, but it is still visible, the shale shards jutting up like a school of shark fins, the tips pocked with the crinoline blooms of lichen that ever so slowly grind the rock down. Wayne has known about these rocks for years. He thinks they are artifacts from Indigenous hunters. The assemblage, at first glance, seems inconsequential, something that could easily be missed in the grander geology of the region, but the slabs of shale, propped in a vertical position, each one similar in weight and size and set an equal distance apart, appear too reflective of a human's patterned purposeful thinking to be coincidental. Too small for a permanent shelter and located on a mountaintop where none of the usual requirements of a camp are available—no trees to block the wind or to provide wood for a fire, no water nearby—Wayne thinks it may have been the site of a spirit quest. I look at the rocks and have no idea what the assemblage means, but I recognize it as a thought-print.

A footprint communicates the way thought and language do. A single track or footprint is like the subject of a sentence. It represents the animal, place or thing. It tells you who was there. But we need more than a subject to complete a thought. We need a predicate as well, an action taken. For tracks to constitute movement, one foot has to make contact twice. If the animal is a biped, three tracks are needed; if a quadruped, five. Now you have a subject and a predicate, a complete thought, a full sentence, a "trackway." Movement and meaning emerge. A trackway will tell you the distance between footsteps. If you have that, you can calculate speed and size of the animal, plus direction of travel, and sometimes, if the track pattern changes, it will tell you whether the animal was moving at a walk, trot, lope or gallop. Whoever positioned the rocks at the top of Bevin Pass in their patterned sequence of shape and size was communicating something too. The tracks they left behind hold the thought-prints of their mind.

When I am on the trail I spend so much time tripping on rocks, using the wrong side of the switchblade, struggling with knots and buckles, that I hardly trust myself. This assemblage of rocks calms me. In their patterned placement, the rocks seem to be saying, *Come now, aren't there some things that you still recognize, some things you still know? Count these rocks. Doesn't one plus one still equal two? Look at their arrangement, doesn't a rectangle still have the same shape?*

The rocks also tell me that another human body looked from the edge of the peak of Bevin Pass, looked across at the mountain ranges just as I am looking now. This particular piece of the planet, still untouched by roads or human industry, is a place where I can gaze as far as possible and, aside from the trail and this arrangement of rocks, not see any evidence of human intervention. Whoever arranged the rocks so many years ago must have seen the same piece of Earth that I see now.

The Earth is a body too. A body that seems indifferent to mine. A branch whacks me in the face. I trip over a rock. The Earth doesn't seem to care if I bruise or bleed. In the same way, my body seems indifferent to me; it bruises and bleeds no matter how much I complain.

Sometimes I think I love the Earth's body more than my own. Maybe it's because it feels more all-knowing, more absolute. Perhaps its separateness serves as that threshold, that still point I crave, the thing that holds each change in my body together. Maybe what I think is that the Earth knows everything about me, and the universe beyond knows everything about the Earth. Like nesting dolls, echoes and reflections reverberating outward in every direction.

SEVEN

Summer of the Horse

It has been over seven years since the day of the book fair where Wayne and I first met. I had imagined a far more leisurely life together, one in which we'd nurture each other's creative pursuits, maybe spend a year at his cabin at Mayfield without ever coming out. But what we did was buy an old farmhouse requiring endless amounts of time and resources, then added two guest houses to accommodate Wayne's clients who come and go, filling my world with so much day-to-day activity that the life I've made for myself bears little resemblance to my original vision.

"Have you seen my notebook?" I say to Wayne. "I need to add *pick up programs* to my list."

"No, I haven't," Wayne says. He folds a dress shirt and lays it in his suitcase.

I stand in the doorway of the bedroom and stare at him. Tomorrow is the start of the Sweetwater 905

Arts and Music Festival, an event that Emilie and I co-founded nearly twenty years ago. What began as a one-night event has now morphed into three days of music, poetry and visual art.

"Timing's not great," I say.

"Tell me about it."

He's off to Vancouver, to a board meeting with the Canadian Parks and Wilderness Society, a position he's held as part of his advocacy work for the Muskwa–Kechika Management Area. He'll attend the meeting tomorrow, fly home the next day, and three days after that he'll head into the M–K on the first leg of the summer's expeditions.

"Rob should be here in a few hours," Wayne says. "I've put the horses who still need to be shod in the pen. When Rob's done, he'll let them back out into the pasture."

Many will say that Rob is the best farrier in the country.

"A hell of a shoer," Wayne agrees, "if you can get him to come when you want."

I know Wayne needs to go to the meeting, but the fact that he's leaving me with the worry of Rob and a host of other tasks related to his summer expedition right when the festival is taking place pisses me off, and I can't stop making it clear. My theory is this: if I don't make it clear, Wayne won't recognize all the compromises I've made, and he'll carry on oblivious. I know the theory is flawed because I think he does recognize the compromises I've made but carries on regardless, possessed of a fervent anti-existentialist way of thinking where nothing exists except the big picture. Give him a medal, is what most people say when they talk about his work to protect the Muskwa–Kechika, a chunk of wilderness the size of Ireland, and I said that too. I suppose I would still say that, given a chance, which is hardly ever because I'm all caught up in the details, cleaning coffee stains from the pine floor, picking up socks, doing laundry, packing groceries into boxes labelled for each leg of his summer expedition, figuring out what I'm going to cook for dinner. Some days I wonder if that's really why Wayne fell for me, because he could see I was possessed of an attention to detail that would allow him to focus on the whole. Of course, if that were true, then he'd probably say that his theory is flawed too, given how cinchy I've become. *Cinchy.* Now there's a word I would never have used before I met Wayne. It means overly sensitive. Touchy. It comes from the experience of tightening the cinch of a saddle so firmly that the horse starts feeling uncomfortable. I make a mental note to add the word to the list of equine phrases I'm collecting in my notebook, expressions like *up on your high horse; don't switch horses midstream; going to see a man about a horse.*

I look at my watch. "I have to go." I give him a hug but it lacks sincerity and as soon as I'm in the car on my way to Emilie's, a few miles west of our place in Rolla, twenty-five miles northeast of Dawson Creek, I feel guilty. Which means I get to add to my list of worries the possibility that Wayne will die in a car or plane crash or maybe get hit on a crosswalk on Robson

Street, and I'll never get to tell him again that I love him. And I do.

At the end of it all, I have only myself to blame. I take on too much and then I gripe about it. I drive into Emilie's yard and just the sight of her, sixty-five years old, wild hair and tight designer jeans, a T-shirt with sequins on it, calms me down. "Sexiest woman around the campfire," is how one cowboy put it at last year's cattle roundup.

Emilie and I met in 1997, at a student art show, when I was living in Bessborough, a forty-minute drive east of Rolla. It was my second year of studies and the instructor had given me my own wall to display my drawings. Emilie attended the show. She was a local celebrity, an artist who took herself seriously. She'd built a studio in her yard, she'd had exhibits of her work and she'd even made a bit of a name for herself for incorporating cow placentas into her sculptures. She looked at my drawings and told me to keep at it, that she liked what I was doing. I couldn't believe how great her comment made me feel. Shortly after, I bought one of her sculptures. It was more than I could afford, so I had to pay for it over time. Which meant that every few weeks I'd drive to her place in Rolla with a cheque, and she'd invite me into her studio, and we'd visit.

One evening during that time, Emilie phoned and asked if I'd come pick her up at the Farmington Store, a gas station and liquor outlet along the Alaska Highway, a few miles east of Bessborough.

"What's up?" I said.

"Larry and I had a spat." On the drive back from the community pasture where Emilie and her husband, Larry, kept their cows over the summer, Larry had kicked Emilie out of the truck. I don't think I ever heard what the argument was about.

When I arrived at the Farmington Store, Emilie was sitting outside on the bank along the highway, the ditch lush with grass and wildflowers, her two collie dogs beside her. She was drinking a cider. She was nonchalant. There were nimbus clouds so black they were turning purple. Thunder and lightning. Emilie opened the back door of my Jeep and the dogs jumped in and she hopped into the front. As we drove along, she told me all the things she liked about me. She said she couldn't understand my insecurities, my blindness to my potential, and the sun knifed through the clouds, an effervescent, apple-bright light. Emilie gave me confidence. She believed in my abilities as a visual artist. Although by then I'd decided I didn't want to be a visual artist. I wanted to be a writer.

"Poetry is what I really want to do," I told Emilie. "I should never have given it up." Which made it sound like it had been a bit of a career at one point, but that wasn't true. I had written poetry, or, more accurately, drivel, when I was a kid. And then, after high school, I'd quit because I thought it was an adolescent pursuit.

Today, when Emilie sees me in the driveway and walks over and we laugh and give each other a hug—a full-bodied embrace that says, thank god we have each other—I feel another twinge of guilt for rushing off without giving Wayne a proper goodbye. Emilie and I go through our checklist. We still have to pick up the programs from the printer and the alcohol for the beer garden, and then we need to get back to the farm to meet the artists who are hanging their work in the barn stalls. I have to get Emilie's studio ready for the poetry readings—there are chairs to set out, a podium to haul from our place, bird shit to mop up from the budgies who fly at large throughout her workspace.

Heady with the success of that first Sweetwater festival, my zeal for organizing had taken off. I began a reading series; I initiated poetry retreats, a writer-in-residence program. In 2000, at a retreat at Moberly Lake, mentor Jan Zwicky gently cautioned me, "You can be an organizer, or you can be a poet. It will be hard for you to be both." At the time, I didn't believe her. I worked part-time at the college. My two children were nearly grown. The poems came easily. I published a book. Then, in 2006, I met Wayne.

In that early flurry of emails he asked, "How would you like to organize an artist retreat in the wilderness?"

The day before Wayne and I met to discuss the retreat, I'd gone for a walk with my family: my husband and two children, my parents, my sister and her family. We'd walked through an evergreen forest on my parents' property. It was winter and there'd been a slight warming period that had drawn out the moisture in objects along the trail, moisture that had then frozen again, forming a skin of ice on dead poplar leaves, encasing a coyote's tooth, moose droppings, objects exquisitely coated in a thin crystallized shell. I remember thinking that I probably wouldn't have noticed these things had they not been transformed by the ice and frost, had they not undergone an elemental change. And how I might not have known that my marriage was over if I hadn't met Wayne.

Now, with every year that passes, I spend less and less time writing. I spend less time in the Muskwa–Kechika as well. As Wayne's business grows, someone needs to be at home to look after the bookkeeping, the logistics of getting people and supplies in and out of the mountains. At this time of year, when Wayne's expedition and the festival are at their peak, I am completely overwhelmed.

Emilie's yard is already a hive of activity. The sound technicians have arrived. People have started to pitch their tents and park their campers in the field behind the mainstage. There's an issue with the merchandise table. We've set it up in the machine shed turned beer garden, underneath the shed's loft. The loft will be used for the VIP lounge; it has a great view of the mainstage, but the locals are up there, Trevor and Wiley, drinking beer and smoking, their cigarette butts falling through the cracks of the plank floor and onto the CDs, T-shirts and the heads of the volunteers.

"No smoking!" Emilie yells at them. "Read the signs! If Larry's shed burns down, I'm done for."

Emilie and I double-check the alcohol order. We drive into town in Emilie's pickup.

"You sure the suspension can take the weight?" asks the woman at the liquor store as we load case after case into the back of Emilie's truck. We pick up the programs and head back to the festival site. The artists have arrived and are hanging their paintings on the rough planks of the barn stalls that will be their gallery for the weekend. Finally, I drive to Fort St. John to get Jeanette Lynes, a poet arriving on a late flight from Saskatoon. It's midnight before we get back home.

Brian Jungen, an artist who has been spending his summer in Rolla, staying in our yard in his camper and helping out with the chores, has been in Grande Prairie all day. I see his vehicle when we pull into the driveway, but he's not in the house, and the camper is dark. Asleep then.

Jeanette and I have a glass of wine in the living room. How wonderful to finally have a few moments with an old friend to talk about writing—*writing*! Jeanette sits on the couch, and I sit facing her on an expansive leather chair that Wayne and I bought cheap because it was used and smelled like cigarette smoke. I sprawl across it, my feet dangling over the edge of its wide arm. I feel so goddamned happy. I gaze, satisfied, at the bookshelves along every wall, shelves that Wayne and I are in constant competition for, and which, over time, Wayne has taken over. My books, though they likely surpass Wayne's in number, are thinner, most of them volumes of poetry. Over the years I have added bookshelves to my office to make more space for Wayne's in the front room. It's a terrible trait I have, one that says sure, go ahead, and then feels bitter about it. On some of the shelves are bones and fossils that Wayne has collected; there's a narwhal tusk on the wall and a mammoth tusk in the corner of the living room and in a curio cabinet—fossils and petrified teeth. *It takes a steady watch, I think, to keep this room from filling with bones.* Jeanette is asking me about our farm. She wants to know what it will mean when Wayne goes away for the summer.

"*Farm* to me means having to get up every morning to do chores," she says.

"Then this isn't really a farm," I assure her. "We rent the land, and this summer the horses who aren't going on the trail are being pastured at the Hutterites'. This summer, besides yard work, I won't have to do chores."

In fact, I have done everything I can to make this summer mine. The horses are pasturing elsewhere so I won't have to pitch hay when the rain doesn't come and the grass dries up; the guests who come and go will be encouraged to fend for themselves in the kitchen. I am a writer, I keep telling myself. I need to write. This summer will be my time to write.

Over the past few days, our house has been filling up with guests. Some are going on Wayne's expedition and some are performing at the festival. With Wayne gone to Vancouver, and people needing places to sleep, I've moved out to the garden shed. Which I'm pleased about because it gives me a place of my own. I've hauled out an air mattress and some bedding. The shed has electricity so there are lights and I can pick up the Wi-Fi to check my email in case there are any last-minute messages from the festival crew. I've brought a kettle of water and a French press so I can have coffee in the morning before having to talk to anyone. I'm jumpy as hell, but being in a place where I feel like no one is going to walk in, where no one is going to ask for something, works like a sedative. I fall asleep. But then, as though some internal hour chimes in me, I wake up at 3:00 a.m. Every night I do this. The dead hour, they say. I have to pee.

I go outside. Solstice is only a few days away; it's light out. Rain has fallen in the night, but it's clear now, the willows and aspen trees glistening, and I can see the horse pasture, mist rising from the wet grass, the air rinsed and bright. Some of the horses are lying down. I stand as still as I can. I tell myself to stop, to soak in the quiet. Soon it will be morning, first day of the festival, and the chaos will begin.

Sometimes, though I don't believe in God, I behave as though I do, thinking I am being shown the error of my ways. *Serves you right,* this God-like thing whispers in my ear, *you wanted too much, you wanted to be a writer, but that wasn't good enough, you wanted to do all these things for other people so you could feel better about yourself, you wanted to leave your husband, you wanted another man, you wanted to go into the wilderness, you didn't care how much pain you'd cause, and now I'll show you, I'll show you, you little floozie, what it's like to never write again.*

I return to the garden shed and sleep. I wake to my alarm—7:00 a.m. I make coffee, check my email. There's one from Wayne, asking how things are going, how the shoeing went—*Can you check the horses?* I leave the garden shed and go into the house. Jeanette is still asleep. I have to get ready to head to the airport to pick up John Barton, another poet performing at the festival. Brian's up and sitting on the couch, checking his email. He says that Wayne has sent him a message too, and that he will check the horses.

I go upstairs to get ready and Brian heads out to the corrals. He opens the gate and sees a pool of blood in the muck of rained-on gumbo. Then blood spattered on the planks of the corral. He thinks something has gotten into the pen and attacked the horses. Then he sees Comet, the big sorrel gelding with a straw-coloured mane, bite marks on his back, hide ripped from the shoulder, the thick leather of it hanging, a drapery of blood and the horse shaking.

I'm brushing my teeth when I hear Brian call my name from the porch.

"Comet's cut up," Brian says when I go to the top of the stairs and look down.

"How bad?"

"Bad."

"Do I call the vet?"

"Yes."

Rob hadn't come. The horses had stayed in the pen all night without food or water and in their restless state had picked on Comet, the lowest horse in their pecking order. Comet must have been pushed against the railing of the pen, because somewhere in the tussle a plank had broken off and a bolt had hooked into his hide and torn him open. Someone should have checked them. Someone should have checked with Rob. That someone was me. I feel nauseous. And it's not because I forgot; it's because, so caught up in the festival and in myself, I hadn't even bothered to add that reminder to my list.

I have to pick up John, leaving Brian to wait for the vet. I don't see the stitching, the tetanus shot, the painkillers, I don't see Brian bring Comet a five-gallon pail filled with water and see Comet drink it all. I don't hear the vet say how lucky Comet is that the wound is where it is: had the injury been lower down on the leg, recovery might have been harder, but with the wound higher up, the horse will live. But not without a lot of care. Comet will need two hosings a day for twenty minutes each for at least two months; he will need ointments and antibiotics. It will take a long time for the wound to heal.

EIGHT

Something about a Horse

One summer on the trail, as the pack string made its way over the alpine ridges from Trimble Lake to the Besa River, all it did was rain, the trail becoming more churned up and harder to navigate as the hours passed, the exposed roots of spruce trees slick as greased metal rods. Wayne could see my energy and the energy of our four guests start to flag. After making a descent into a narrow valley with just enough trees for shelter and just enough grass for the horses, he decided to stop early and set up camp. Cold and wet, our group sat scrunched in a strip of spruce and poplar along the steep bank of a creek around a fire that smoked more than it flamed. The horses grazed nearby. I couldn't wait to be done with the dinner and the dishes and crawl into the dry tent. Once inside our sleeping bags, the warmth of Wayne's body was a life raft I clung to as the rain pelted down.

There was a risk that the horses would grow restless with their small patch of grass and decide to travel back over the mountain in search of better food, so we slept lightly—listening for the clanking of the horse bells that marked their grazing. At 5:00 a.m., Wayne heard the bells' clappers quicken. "The horses are heading out," he said, waking me. He was already getting dressed. I sat up and watched him leave the tent.

I wriggled into my pants, the bottoms still damp, pulled on my gumboots, gritted my chattering teeth. Once outside, I could see that Wayne had already caught Hazel, the horse who came up with the big ideas that the rest then followed, and was leading her back to camp, sucking most of the horses back down with her.

Wayne's trips are experiential. "Do not expect a typical 'tourist' trip," is what his brochures will tell you. "Expect to be treated as an expedition member and fellow traveller." But this morning there wasn't time to wake the guests up. With the rain lashing down, it was up to me and Wayne to get the other horses tied up. I gathered a few of the halters and moved through the trees by the creek, the branches of wet willows slapping against me, the shallow dish of their leaves tipping water down my neck. I heard a crack of thunder and then the low, muffled rumble of a jet engine. I imagined the passengers up in the plane, warm and dry in their seats, perhaps a woman with a neck pillow ordering a mai tai, heading to Maui.

I spotted Tuchodi by the bank—a hummock of black, the warmth of his hide steaming from the rain. I hesitated. A Percheron cross, Tuchodi was one of the biggest pack horses in Wayne's string. He was also one of the most excitable and nervous. I was not confident catching him. But I knew that the longer it took to catch the horses, the longer it would be before I could stand beside the fire and warm up. As I drew near, I focused on a patch of Tuchodi's black mane, made it the only thing that existed in the mist of steam and breath. *Be the mane.* I fixed my mind on it, and it was as if I'd clasped a tuft of his thick sweep of hair before my hand made contact with it. Believing I could grasp Tuchodi's mane seemed to help my ability to achieve it. Wayne would say it was because I exuded confidence. I had reined in my insecurities, taken control of my doubting mind and in so doing, had taken control of Tuchodi's mind as well. Recognizing my confidence, Tuchodi accepted me as his leader and stayed put. Whatever it was, it worked. I reached up on my tiptoes and brought the crown strap over his crested neck, then slipped Tuchodi's muzzle between the cheek pieces and did up the buckle.

Some people say you should put the lead rope over the horse's neck before you start to put the halter on. Some say you should lead by walking at the horse's shoulder. On the trail, you need to walk directly in front, a few feet of lead rope between you and the horse so there's space for the horse to clamber up hills and over rocks behind you. Some say you should be at ease on a horse. Others say no matter how long you've been riding, you should always be alert to what might go wrong.

Wayne says we view horses as if we are looking in a mirror—horses are a reflection of our own character. If we like to be in control, then we think the horse is there to be controlled. If we want a horse to be our friend, we think a horse is there to be our friend. Wayne is largely prosaic; he thinks horses are tools. Which doesn't mean that he thinks they don't have feelings or needs, but he sees a horse as an animal that, through years of domestication, of selection and culling, has become a useful aid. I am an unconfident, anxious human having a hard time believing I should be in control of another animal. People tell me that horses would be less afraid if they knew I was in charge. Not possible, is what I say. First, I'm not confident, and a horse will know that. And who am I to say when a horse is more or less afraid than me? Can a horse adapt to a rider's fear? Can we still ride in consensual joy? I don't know. I've spent most of my time riding in a pack string where the horses follow each other and know where they are going. There's not a lot I have to ask the horse to do.

Ray Hunt, one of the original proponents of natural horsemanship, a method that seeks to create a rapport with a horse, also uses the mirror as a metaphor for the horse, suggesting that when he looks at a horse, he sees the rider too.

Maybe it's as simple as saying that how you treat a horse will affect the way a horse treats you. A horse becomes a reflection of our character through our interaction with it. But what is it about a horse that makes it so willing to absorb us, to allow us to change the way it behaves?

The evolutionary physiologist and geographer Jared Diamond, in *Guns, Germs, and Steel*, lists the six criteria that animals must meet for domestication. They can't be strict carnivores—it's too economically inefficient to feed a picky eater. They must mature quickly relative to us. They must be willing to breed in captivity. They can't have "nasty dispositions"—they can't want to eat you. They can't be flighty. Animals who panic easily and flee are hard to control. Finally, they should be herd-bound. They need to recognize you as their leader.

Horses fit these criteria, and thousands of years ago humans began to breed the horses who demonstrated those qualities best, culling the ones who didn't.

In a 2014 email, writer Luanne Armstrong said:

It is actually amazing how few animals will accept or have accepted domestication. And horses are weird. What is in it for them? They go wild easily, almost instantly. All that is in domestication for them is basically abuse. And yet they seem to almost crave contact with people. After sixty years, I still can't understand it. Why, after two hours of riding my horse in circles, does he lean the whole weight of his head on me and stand there and just breathe. It is actually terrifying to have him give me that trust.

Wayne likes to take the long view. He sees human intervention with animals as a natural outcome of evolution, what he calls "selective pressure." Not unlike the way ants domesticate aphids: biting off the aphids' wings or excreting chemicals to keep them dozy, ants have learned to keep the insects close, milking them for their dew, and, in return, protecting the aphids from their predators. In this kind of domestication there rises a co-evolution.

We are drawn to horses and horses are drawn to us.

I remember the first time I heard the term *sit a horse*. The words came from a guest going on one of Wayne's expeditions. It was during a party I'd thrown for her so she could meet the locals, and so I wouldn't have to entertain her on my own. We were sitting around the kitchen table, an old piece of furniture we'd bought at a second-hand store and once painted yellow, then crudely sanded back down. I'd covered it with a red-and-yellow-checked cloth. I remember that because, in discussing the trip the guest was about to go on, the inevitable question arose—"Are you a horse person?"—and she replied, "I'm not an expert rider, but I do know how to sit a horse." It was a flashbulb moment, like when I heard Elvis Presley had died. Now, whenever I hear the phrase, I think of the guest, the tablecloth, me in my red sleeveless shirt.

How firmly the dropped preposition put her in possession of the horse, how unequivocally it transformed the horse into an object to be acted on. When I told Wayne I didn't like the phrase, he said, "How come?"

"It sounds pretentious."

"Maybe that's because you're not used to the term."

"No, no. It's something else." I tried to think of what that something else might be. "Okay," I said, "if I say I'm going to hike on Bevin Pass, there is a kind of meandering implied, a willy-nilly nature to the hike. But if I say I'm going to hike Bevin Pass, it suggests a beginning and an end that I am in control of."

I've heard riders talk about communicating with their horse in a way that gives rise to an intuitive back-and-forthing, a co-being in which the horse and rider anticipate each other's movements, even each other's thoughts. I wonder if it's a bit like the two-step.

I learned this simple dance by standing on my father's feet as we moved around the living room to songs like "The Cowboy in a Continental Suit." While some dancers lead with their mind, following the two-step rule of *quick, quick, slow,* my father used the steps of the dance as loose scaffolding behind the rhythm of each song. The difference between the two approaches has always seemed profound. To dance with someone who leads with an intuitive sense of the music seems to give entry to the very emotion and spirit of a body's engagement with life. At those times I am more than willing, eager even, to follow. My body's movements are drawn into the rhythm of my partner's body and the movements of my partner's body are drawn into mine. We move in an intensified joy.

Maybe a rider moving in sync with a horse creates, for both, a rapport of trust and an intensified engagement with life. Maybe if you're a really good rider, the horse is happy to follow. Maybe, at some point, the lead is mutual.

The mind and the body are both dancers too. In my case, too often both try to lead. Neither one trusts the other. The two do not ride in consensual joy. My mind becomes nervous and my body stumbles.

Some take the view that consciousness is an epiphenomenon, the result of enough neurons in the brain firing to reach a boiling point the way a pot of water reaches a boil and produces steam. With this theory, consciousness may be superfluous, but still important. After all, steam may be an emergent property of boiling water, but it is the steam, not the boiling water, that shapes the brim of a cowboy hat, unseals an envelope, powers the engine of a train. It is consciousness that tells me who I am.

A domesticated horse may be an emergent property of the modifications we've made through selective breeding—an animal that reflects our desires, just as consciousness reflects the brain's activities—but the instant I walk away from a horse, he returns to his essential horseness. As Luanne Armstrong says, "Horses go wild easily, almost instantly."

Sometimes I like to think of consciousness this way: it is something my brain domesticates, reins in from some cosmic field. My mind a wild thing. When I die, consciousness will be let out of its corral, returned to its own essential horseness, as Tuchodi, when we're done for the day, turns away from me, bending his broad forehead to the ground, his whiskered muzzle winnowing through a patch of lupines, his muscled ears swivelling, the rims of his nostrils stiffening in the flare, his hide rippling at the touch of a fly, his spirit surging his body across the plain.

Comet, in the summer before his injury, mills with the rest of the herd at the end of a trail day.

NINE

Comet

After I return from the airport with John, I put on my gumboots and go out to look at Comet. I figure if I spread out my hands, it would take fifteen of them to cover Comet's wound. And where the wound is deepest, where the muscles are cut and exposed, is a hollow so deep that if I lifted the hide to fully expose it, I think I could stick my head inside.

"Horses have a lot of mass," Emilie says when she comes over for a look. "It's not as bad as it seems."

"Good," I say. "Because it looks like the horse will die."

Before I met Wayne, Emilie and I didn't talk about horses. We might be outside, even walking through her horse pasture, but the interests we shared were more toward art and relationships. We were "figuring out life," as Emilie likes to say, "like we are sane or something."

Before I decided to leave my husband and before Emilie decided to stay with hers, she used to say we were on the same journey, that we kept each other afloat. She doesn't say that as often now. Even though we live nearly next door to each other and horses have become, by necessity, a part of my life and, by passion, have always been a part of hers, I think she sees me on a slightly different vessel, one in which we no longer share the same bail bucket.

Emilie was eleven when she got her first horse.

"And you wanted the horse," I say. "It wasn't someone else's idea?"

"Oh, god no, I wanted a horse since I could ever remember. I was real little."

"How did you know you wanted a horse?"

"Don't you always know when you want something?"

I think of Plato's allegory of the cave, how if we were born chained to one spot with only a blank wall in front of us, we'd have no thoughts at all. You can't know what something is if you don't know what it isn't.

"Well," I say, "you can't want something you've never known."

"Well, then, I saw a horse. The first horse I saw that I remember was when I was about four. It was at the relatives' and they put me on this pony and apparently I wasn't afraid, but they took me off because I didn't want my brother on it. I remember being a little bruised up about that because I was riding in the front and Brian was riding behind me, he was a year younger, and we were trotting around in this little fenced area, it was probably very tiny, but you know when you're a kid it's huge, and then they took the pony away because I wouldn't share it. I was kicking up a bit and it would go beyond a walk and my brother would fall off and that wasn't good. That's the first time I remember riding a pony."

"You did that on purpose, to get him to fall off?"

"No, I wasn't trying to make him fall off, I just wanted to go faster. And I didn't care if he fell off—it was the consequence of going faster. Anyway, they took the pony away. That was the start and after that I always wanted a horse and I finally got one."

Anyone who has seen Emilie on a horse will say it's a beautiful thing, a muscled union of animated energy.

There are antibiotics that Comet will need to take orally for ten days. Fly repellent to be applied around the outer rim of the wound. Fura-Zone to the wound itself and a salve to be used in case the Fura-Zone runs down Comet's leg and creates a rash. The hosing is to begin right away.

When Wayne acquired Comet, the owner told me, "It's a man's horse." *Try telling Emilie that*, is what I'd thought at the time, but I'd kept my mouth shut. What irked me wasn't just the implication in his remark that a man could handle a horse better than a woman; it was also that, as with so many things that bug me, I felt an undercurrent of worry that it could be true. And now? Hosing a "man's horse," a horse I am in no way comfortable with, twice a day, all summer long?

Brian has already strung garden hoses together so they reach the corral where Comet is to be confined. Brian can see my hesitation. He hands me the hose. He's attached my watering wand to the end of the hose and my first thought is, *That's my expensive watering wand!*

"You may as well start now," he says. "You're the one who will be doing this." And it's true. When Wayne's expedition leaves in a few days, Brian is going too. What did I know about wounded horses? What did I know about horses at all?

"There goes my summer," I say to Wayne when he returns from Vancouver, just a few days before he'll hit the trail. And as always when I complain, he nods. Wayne is always sympathetic. Also, not once has he suggested that this might not have happened had I bothered to check the horses. In fact, I have never heard Wayne place blame on anyone. I have never heard him speak ill about another being, human or otherwise. I wish I could say the same for myself.

"Well, what should we do about it?" he says.

And as always, I don't know. On the face of it, the answer is simple. I can't be with Wayne and remain disconnected from how he makes his living. As long as I live in this house, I am a part of what goes on. I can leave or I can stay, and I don't want to leave.

I don't want Emilie to take care of Comet, either. Which she's offered to do.

"Why don't you bring him to my place," she'd said. "The grandkids will be coming and going all summer. They'd love to help."

I have my mother's stubborn pride. Maybe I don't want Emilie to see me give up. Maybe I enjoy being a martyr, which has been suggested a time or two. "You need to be more generous," Wayne has said when I've refused someone's offer to assist. Maybe I need to prove I can do this. Maybe, and this is the thought that settles inside me, maybe I'm curious to know what it is to heal a wound.

The expedition ascends Steeple Pass.

TEN

Hitting the Trail

The morning on which Wayne heads into the hills is one of excitement and organized chaos. The stock truck comes at 7:00 a.m., and the guests and the wranglers pitch in with loading the horses, the saddles, tack and panniers. Meanwhile I'm in the house cleaning up from breakfast, packing up the night's dinner, checking to see if the irrigation is turned off, if anything is plugged in that shouldn't be, noting the ball cap and phone charger left behind by one of the guests, making sure the cats haven't been locked inside a room. When the stock trailer leaves, everyone, including me, who will go up to help with the send-off, needs to be ready to follow. Emilie has offered to take care of Comet until I return.

This year the trailhead is the dilapidated parking lot of the Summit Lake Lodge, 392 miles up the Alaska Highway. Fifty years ago, when the roads weren't paved and vehicles were less fuel efficient, there were lodges like this one all along the highway. Cinnamon buns and coffee were their claim to fame. Today the main building of the Summit Lake Lodge and all of the accompanying cabins, once painted a bright turquoise, have been abandoned, the paint faded and peeled, most of the windows smashed.

By the time we arrive, it's late afternoon. The stock trailer is there, the horses inside loose but separated by gates according to who gets along with whom. They've been inside for nearly eight hours. They're restless, jostling for position, the clattering of their shod feet against the metal floor amplifying the size of their bodies. Terry, the stock truck driver, opens the back door and he and Wayne, armed with halters, slip inside, then shut the door behind them. The clattering accentuates. It is as though Wayne and Terry are magicians going into a secret vault, the noise a kind of mysterious shuffling of a metallic deck, and then voila, the door opens, and one by one the horses leap out.

Please give me Hazel, is what I would pray those first few years. *Please don't give me Gataga or Tuchodi— they are humongous and way too spirited!* We grab the lead ropes of the horses' halters as they jump from the stock truck. We lead them toward a patch of trees and tie them up. Their nostrils widen, taut as rubber sealing rings, as they breathe in their new surroundings, glad to be out of the trailer but nervous, filled with a bristling energy.

After a few years, something in me said, *Okay, I can do this. Gataga, I know you, and what I know is that at heart, you are a kind soul.* But the act of leading a horse still feels like a trick to me, even at times a sort of showing off: See how I can handle the more energetic horses? Isn't it something, the way they trust me? When all of the horses are out of the trailer and tied to the trunks of the aspen and spruce, we loosen their lead ropes so their heads can reach the ground to eat the flakes of hay that we break from the square bales we've brought. As we disburse the food, the horses whinny—*Over here, over here! I'm starving!*

We pitch our tents and spend the night in the old campground area, but sleep is restless. Wayne gets up several times to check the horses. Sometime near dawn—I've been dreaming so can't be sure—I wake to Wayne's hand on my thigh. It feels warm and solid, full of attention and hope, a kind of comfort edged with relief. We have not been spending time together, or, when we have, it's been to balance books or cook dinner for the guests who've flowed in and out of our home.

"I wish you were coming with me," Wayne will say, but after seven years, we both know, or should, that it's not true. Who would stay home to keep the lawn mowed, the flowers watered and weeded? Who would relay the messages back and forth between Wayne and his clients? Who would host and feed those clients on their way up then back down the highway?

While the first leg of each summer's expeditions has the added logistics of getting the horses—this year there are twenty-one—and their gear to the trailhead, getting guests in and out of each subsequent leg is like trying to solve a distance/time/speed problem. For example, two weeks from now, on a Thursday, Mary will drive into Rolla in her own vehicle. On Friday, John and Eric will fly into Fort St. John (45 minutes north of Rolla). On Saturday, Mary will head north to Fort St. John and pick up John and Eric at the Northern Grand. The three will travel two hours farther north to Sasquatch Crossing where they will pick up Melodie's vehicle, which was left in the dusty parking lot two weeks prior from when the first set of guests rode in off the highway. John will drive Melodie's vehicle and the three will convoy to Fort Nelson. On Sunday, these three, along with three more who have flown directly into Fort Nelson, will fly by bush plane into the head of the Prophet River for the second leg of the expedition. The guests from the first leg will fly out, including Melodie, and together they will drive Melodie's and Mary's vehicles back to Fort St. John. How will Mary's vehicle get back to Fort Nelson?

The answer? Wayne needs me more in Rolla than on the trail.

But it isn't just the yard and the expediting and the hosting and now Comet that keep me home. My father isn't well. He hasn't been for some time, but lately he seems to be getting worse.

A few years ago, the pain in my father's hip became too much to bear, which must have been significant, because (a) my father rarely complained, and (b) he hated to go to the doctor. He finally did go, and the doctor discovered that my dad, at seventy-six, needed a hip replacement. They also discovered that his blood pressure was through the roof, and that it had likely been that way for a very long time. So along with the worn-out hip, my father had acquired congestive heart failure. In a matter of a few months he had a hip replacement and a pacemaker. These operations did not go well, and life as he'd known it—a life spent outdoors, farming and roaming the woods nearby— was over.

As soon as my father came out of his hip surgery, we could see a change. At first it was minor confusions, getting names of people mixed up. We put it down to the anaesthetic. With time, we told ourselves, he would improve. Then there were moments when he'd stop in his tracks as if he'd forgotten where he was. It happened swiftly. In what seemed a matter of weeks, he'd gone from sitting at my kitchen table, talking about politics and railroad subsidies, to forgetting how to fix a tire on his tractor. He'd always said, "Donna, if I ever get so I don't know who I am, put a pillow over my face."

By the summer of Comet's wound, at the age of eighty-two, my dad was in full-blown dementia. It was getting harder for my mom to care for him. I hated to be away for more than a few days at a time. Doctors had done brain scans and confirmed that my father had, over the past few years, been having small strokes—TIAs, transient ischemic attacks—and with each one, he diminished a little more.

I lie there in the pre-dawn light, half asleep, listening to Wayne breathe, trying to imprint this moment of calm in my brain, hoping for it to become a memory that will sustain me for the next few months. I think back to our first summer together on the trail. I think of my family. I think too of the wounded horse.

It takes several hours to pack up in the morning, a slow building up to the moment when Wayne and his crew will ride off. After breakfast, the coffee cups and dishes are washed, stacked just so in the dish basin, the kettle and grills slipped into their respective storage bags, then put into the panniers. Tents and sleeping gear are laid out on tarps that will be turned into soft packs for the horses to carry. The horses are saddled, stirrups adjusted for their riders, adjusted again, demos here, demos there, the bridles put on. People make their lunches, then stow them along with cameras and binoculars in their saddlebags; they tie their rain gear and warm coats behind their saddles. With each passing day, this moving becomes more efficient. On the first day of the trail, the takeoff time is always near noon, but by the end of each expedition, the time will have shortened by several hours.

The string is packed in a particular order, having to do with which horse gets the heavier load as well as with how well behaved they are. The trick is to keep them all together, to not have one striking out before it is time. The less compliant pack horses are kept tied to trees until the end, but the others are free to mill around, their cargo swaying back and forth as they wait for Wayne to get on Bonus, to hear him say—drawing out the *L*—"Let's go." When the last horse is being packed, everyone needs to be in his or her saddle. Here is when someone might realize they need to pee or they can't find their hat. Urgency rises.

"There's a lot of moving parts," Wayne says. And all those moving parts have to coalesce and move as one unit. If there's a misstep—*Wait! Kylo is still tied up!*—and things pause, some of the horses will start off on their own and often in the wrong direction. There is no time for a proper goodbye; that should have been done hours ago. Instead, it's a quick wave and "I love you!" shouted over the backs of the horses and riders as they trot away. I watch them disappear into the trees. It takes a few moments for the quiet to descend, but when it does its weight is palpable. So much movement and so much energy and now all of it gone. The pack string and the riders are off on their adventure where, on each travel day, they will cover an average of ten miles, where even now they are discovering the trail, bonding together without me.

I stand in the empty campsite like a returnee from Oz, the place gone back to abandoned. I walk around, looking for anything that might have been left in the flurry of the pack string's leaving. I get in the Blazer, the back seat filled with a jumble of coolers and backpacks and water bottles and the unwashed pot from last night's chili. I turn the key in the ignition and head back home.

Members of the artist camp, having set out at dawn, reach the alpine at mid-afternoon. SHEILA PETERS

ELEVEN

A Secret to Tell

Have you ever been lost?" I asked Wayne, when we first met. "No," he said, "I always knew how to get back to where I started."

"Are we lost now?" I asked, a few weeks later.

During that first summer at Mayfield, I was determined to not lose my sense of direction. That, at least, by god, was a skill I'd come equipped with. But what I think is the ridge, isn't. Ahead is another rise, and now the hail has come and in sheets, and only now does it occur to me that when I'd climbed to the top of the mountain I should have looked across the valley and picked a far-off peak as a marker and positioned our camp below in relation to it. The marker I had eyed up, a particular boulder at the top of a rise, is now just one of a hundred erratics peppering the alpine, the hail obliterating the trail formed by caribou and sheep, filling the crushed-shale dent of the animals' steps until everything is lost.

I know north from south. I know camp is north. But when I do reach the ridge and look down, the lake where we have camped, a tarn on the shoulder of the mountain, is gone. I can see a lake below, but not our bright-petalled tents. I must have walked too far east and here, can you believe it, is a second lake. How off-course am I? How far east could I have possibly gone?

Wayne cannot find out. That's the first thing. If he does, it will be the second time he'll have thought I was lost. And that bothers me, that he assumes I have no navigation skills. The first time Wayne assumed I couldn't find my way through the bush was at his base camp at Mayfield Lake. We'd gone to get the horses. We'd studied the horses' shod tracks along the trail, assessed the freshness of the horse droppings, stopped every now and then to listen for their bells and found the herd several miles northwest of Wayne's cabin. They were milling around, eighteen in all this year, swishing their tails, fighting flies on a sandbar across a backwater channel of the Gataga River. We took off our shoes, our socks, our jeans and, balling our clothes into our arms, we waded across the stream. Once we'd made it to the sandbar, Wayne unhobbled the horses.

I was still getting used to riding a horse with a saddle, much less riding bareback. I watched the horses leap about, their shod feet big as saucers, huge Percheron crosses full of energy and vigour, and decided I'd rather be on foot. Once Wayne realized he couldn't change my mind, he got on his horse Bonus and I waded back across. When we reached the other side, he got off and haltered Hazel, the quiet, über-compliant sorrel mare who, because of these traits, was most often stuck with the beginners who came on the trail. Wayne handed me her lead rope, the plan being that I would walk with Hazel behind Wayne and the rest of the horses would follow. When we began to wind through a patch of willow and poplar and Hazel could see that I didn't know how to lead a horse, and that all of the other horses were crashing through the trees and passing her, she tried to shake me, and I let her. She showed a wild streak I hadn't seen before and haven't seen since as she bolted away, lead rope dangling, panicked at being left behind, knocking me into the willows, then thundering after Wayne and the rest of the horses. Stumbling back out of the brush, I found myself in the same patch of moss and rock we'd stopped at on our way to the horses. It was where Wayne had showed me the *Pinguicula vulgaris*, common butterwort. *Amazing*, is what I'd thought at the time, but in the eerie quiet of being left behind, the squat, no-frills meat-eating wonders took on a more sinister air.

Not for a moment did I think I was lost.

It is true that I ended up walking the way the crow flies, so there were times when I'd come to a deep creek and, anxious to get back to camp, and not knowing how far I'd have to travel up or down before finding a narrow place to cross, I would plunge right in. In one spot, the water rose to my chest and I had just the slightest nagging sensation that my choice might have been less than brilliant. And for sure once I reached the forest where the fire had passed through that spring, I struggled over deadfall I didn't need to because I had forgotten exactly where the trail was, but as I clambered about, ashes glued to my wet jeans, stiffening them, I always knew which way I was going. Up through the burn I marched, past cup fungus letting off spores like ghosts of smoke, and when I reached the lake I turned left to the hand-hewn log cabin where Wayne wasn't.

I remember thinking that somehow I'd beaten him back. But after a few minutes, another thought occurred. Maybe Wayne was looking for me. I left my red backpack by the door of the cabin as a sign that I was not lost, then headed back toward the burn. Partway through I heard a horse bell and I followed its sound, expecting to meet Wayne and the horses. But when I saw him, it was just Wayne. He'd let the horses go and was winding his way, back and forth, up and down the burn. My heart pulled a little when I saw his solitary figure swinging a horse bell, its ring a signal to me. On one hand, I was offended that he had so little faith in me, but on the other, I knew that if he'd just carried on, if he'd ridden to camp and left me behind, I might have wondered how much he cared. In that first summer together, adjusting to our new relationship, I'm sure there were times when we both felt utterly alone.

When I saw the tension in Wayne's face relax into a look of wild relief I realized that while it had never crossed my mind that I might have been lost, for Wayne it had been a distinct possibility. And then another realization crept in—I was in a part of the world where I'd have to travel many miles on foot or horse across rivers and over mountain passes if I were ever to see the Alaska Highway again. And while it was true that I'd found my way back to Mayfield Lake, it was also true that the lake was the only landmark I knew. Wayne must have known this too.

I tried to snuff out my newfound unease. I didn't know how to ride a horse or chop wood or do a diamond hitch, but by god I knew how to be in the bush. It is where I'd grown up, on the banks of the Kiskatinaw River. As a child, I'd often sleep outside where bears and coyotes roamed. And later, with my own children, we'd wander the wooded areas with a deep familiarity. Never, in my entire life, had I ever been lost. But until I'd met Wayne, I'd never really moved from the place where I was born. In fact, I'd lived in the same area so long I hadn't even learned the names of the grasses or the flowers or the trees. It was as if the names weren't necessary; they were a part of the body I'd been born into. I knew them in a different, more intrinsic way.

It's occurring to me now, up in the alpine, the hail plastering me, and my shirt and jeans getting drenched, that the impulse to name just might originate in being lost. We name in order to be a part of an unfamiliar world, to gain a sense of control. I keenly wanted to be in control. But I wasn't. My body was bolting just as Hazel had done. Everything it was doing—heart pounding, hands shaking—seemed out of my control. *I am lost. I am. Calm yourself. You are not lost. Bewildered. Disoriented. Not lost.*

When we'd gone to get the horses, and when we'd first taken off with me leading Hazel behind Wayne, he'd suggested something about trying not to get separated. I'd waved him off, slighted at being talked to like a child. This time, also, up on the alpine, as we waited for the others in our crew to assemble, Wayne had advised me not to head back alone. But I'd insisted, the storm barrelling toward us and me without a coat, and also, a part of me wanted to head back just to prove I could, to emphasize I had never been lost, not with the horses, not ever.

And where was Wayne anyway? On some rise I could no longer find, gathering up the rest of the crew. "Wayne," I yell. "Wayne!" I call it out in one direction and then in another. He must have passed me. Somewhere, at some point, we had to have been just a few feet apart; we just didn't know.

The hail is coming down harder than ever, and for a few minutes the landscape disappears. It's a mountain but it's flat as a plain. I can't see a fucking thing. They say getting lost in the mountains is harder than on the prairies because, in the mountains, there are so many landmarks to steer by. But you have to be alert to those landmarks, you have to watch for things you've seen before, you have to have established points of reference.

Wade Davis, in *The Wayfinders*, writes of the ancient Polynesians who could navigate their canoes in the dark, feeling their way through the water. They could tell the difference between waves created by local weather and those formed by distant pressure systems. They could tell by the way the waves lapped against the canoe which island they were getting close to. They paid attention. Whereas I am seized with a panic so wild and alive, I feel outside of myself. Oh, for the flat-faced axe blade of my own kind!

And then, out of the blue, in the worst possible way, I need to relieve myself. I duck out of sight, which is crazy because if someone were to see me it would mean I'd been found. Here, without any reference points, I am my own place. I am on my own. The only footing is me. And I don't trust myself.

Pull yourself together, Donna. I do know which way is east and which way is west. For instance, if I walk far enough west, I should be able to look down and see Mayfield Lake. So that's what I do. I walk west. I walk until I can see over the edge of the mountain, and there, down below—Mayfield Lake.

It is as if the lake is proof of me, the way my body settles. And then, because I know we travelled the game trail from Mayfield up the flank of the mountain, I slip down the scree, praying, though I don't believe in God, that soon I'll see the trail, and yes, I see it, the trail with hoofprints of the shod horses and here and there, day-old horse droppings. *Thank you, thank you, thank you!* And what kind of story might fly? Something to suggest I was never worried, that my body was never spooked? "Oh," I will say, "I was never lost. I always knew where I came from."

Maybe, if I pick up my pace, I'll get back to the tarn and no one will ever know. But there he is, Wayne, striding toward me, carrying a huge bag over his shoulder, that same wild look of relief on his face.

"What's in the bag?" I say, trying for nonchalance.

"Survival gear."

We walk back to camp, strange animals following a trail made by other animals. We are quiet. Some fine cartilage is building, a connective tissue laying its foundation inside us. A history, a story to tell.

When we get back to camp everyone makes much of me and my drenched body. It turns out there was a second lake, but it was hidden in a fold of the mountain and could only be seen from farther west. The lake I saw had to have been the lake we were camped at. I don't know why I didn't see the tents. Maybe my fierce refusal to be lost ensured I was.

After I've changed my clothes and warmed up by the fire, I look up at the place where I was—not lost—bewildered. But that's not right. I was lost. I might have known how to get back to where I came from, but I had no idea where I was. I would never be able to find the particular dips and hollows where I spooked myself. My fingers stiff with cold, I feel like an exchange has been made—inside me a part of the alpine still clings, unnameable in its strangeness. And in the alpine, a part of me remains, still trying to find my way home.

TWELVE

A Memory of My Father

The mosaic of red and grey tiles that walled the exterior of the Co-op glinted in the light of a late-day sun. The tiles looked waxed, as richly lustred as my patent leather shoes with a daisy on each toe, the petals a deep blue plastic. I was a skinny, freckle-faced girl with red hair now inside the store, in Giftware, standing beside my father on bits of broken glass as the farmers' wives pushed their carts up and down the grocery aisles, buying their weekly supply of sliced bread, perhaps a ham hock or turkey, cans of peaches, tins of sardines, just as they had been doing for over fifty years—a place where the cashiers knew the elderly patrons' membership numbers by heart.

What my father had meant to do was pick up the glass canister and call it fancy, but what he did was hold it by its wooden lid so the canister unsuctioned and fell to the floor. It is likely that my mother, waiting in Clothing, distractedly sifting through the racks of blouses, thinking *Canisters, for heaven's sake, why is this so hard for him,* jumped at the sudden noise but then grew deathly still.

On a day when grain prices fluctuated and the humidity of the wheat kernels in the granary were in question, my father and I stood, thousands of shards of broken glass at our feet, my father's tanned face gone ruddy, the pearl snaps of his wrangler shirt buttoned to his throat. The astonishment on his face reminded me of another spring day when the two of us had looked at my mother in the opened door of our farmhouse, the scattered stems of dandelions weeping their milk into the gravel, my mother standing in the doorway with her arms outspread, having flung the fine yellow-strapped blossoms to the ground. I was baffled, waiting for reason to fit like the bright coloured blocks shaped as stars, squares and circles that slotted into the holes of the plastic ball I often played with, the pleasant clunk-drop of things gone as planned.

Store-bought flowers were what my mother had wanted. How could he give her weeds, she had said. In the wilted air of disappointment, I considered my father, how we'd walked from the pasture, lighthearted at sighting the first spring flower beside the fence post. The gesture gone wrong. And this time, too, my mother's birthday canister, bits of glass scattering like a surprised flock of starlings lifting from the wheat-yellow stubble startling me and my father, as we'd been startled by the thrown dandelions, my mother picking them back up from the dirt, saying she was sorry, only she looked hurt.

I tried not to look at my father, whose gaze had turned toward the bench just inside the entrance of the Co-op, where, seated tightly beside each other, their thighs touching while their wives did the shopping, the men might be discussing the Crow rate, the bushels per acre of barley, and always the weather forecast they'd heard on the radio or noted by the cloud patterns in the sky.

I heard the clerk talking. She was saying there was blood on my father's hand from the canister that had gone from shaped glass to a spray of shrapnel. I could see how my father's shame had grazed and wounded him, his shyness allowing nothing but breath from his mouth. I wished I could have put my hand under the jar and caught it before it fell. That was the moment I knew how carefully my mother must have worked to hide the difference between what appeared—"Look at the canister my husband has bought me for my birthday"—and what was: a husband so shy he could hardly enter a store. I flamed with the knowledge that my mother had given me this task, to take my father to Giftware to buy the canister while she pretended to be elsewhere, a task intended to ease my father's annual chore, my mother watching the clock on the wall, her hands touching the blouses on the rack in the clothing aisle, gestures meant to give space for us to buy the birthday gift, a task that had failed, my father holding the wooden lid and the glass jar smashed to bits.

Bit by bit, the world loses its shine. I saw my father's humiliation and felt a hurt I couldn't name. I wanted rid of the shyness that came with broken canisters, a hovering clerk addressing the cut on my father's hand; I wanted gone the shards of glass, the awkward silence that spread like frost, wanted back the shyness that came without shame and letdowns, a shyness inseparable from that gentle light in which my father would play the banjo on rainy afternoons and I'd curl up beside him, feel the vibration of the instrument against my small bones, the heat of his tanned arm, the gentleness when once, having moved a bale of hay with his tractor, my father had stopped the tractor and gotten off, then in the curve of his palm lifted a pink macaroni noodle—the baby weasel that had fallen from a nest in the crook of another bale—and laid it back in its nest with such luxurious care the memory of it makes me ache.

Now my father was in the hands of strangers, in the hands of the clerk and the janitorial staff who were cleaning up the jar he had broken, swooping down to pick up a piece of glass that I'd kicked, scuffing the toe of my patent leather shoe; employees who only wanted to be helpful, to pick up the shards of glass that would never be pieced back together. But my father would not speak.

Back in our living room, my father playing the banjo, my small body feeling again the tremors of the music, his gentle light returned. But it was an altered light—it was not the innocent shyness of before. It had the taint of inferiority. The memory of the broken glass had put a flaw in it. It was not the shyness from which beauty comes; it was the shyness that is the wizened seed of things unconfronted.

On some future spring morning I will feel restless with my shards of memory, the serrated shapes that didn't fit then worn down by hopes since realized or dashed, experiences lustred then dulled, the glint and unglint of each conglomerate day. I will feel a pinprick of sadness, but the moment will be quick to rub against others so its distinction wears away. It will not graze or wound as before, this childhood thing, this wish for perfection, but something—might it be wisdom?—will have settled in. Something I could never, at that long-ago moment, have accounted for, though surely it had begun even then.

I ready myself for the challenge of Bucky.

THIRTEEN

First Day on Comet's Trail

In order to hose Comet before I go to work each morning I have to set my alarm for 6:00 a.m. The irony of keeping trail time when I'm at home is not lost on me: it's one more tick on the list of all the travesties made against the summer I thought would be mine. But I know the indignity I feel is really borne of something else—I don't want to be responsible for Comet's demise. I am terrified I will fail.

One good thing about my anxiety is that when the alarm goes off, the adrenalin rush of my fear makes it easier to get out of bed. I look out the window. Not a cloud in the sky, the morning light touching the blades of grass, the leaves of the weeping birch, as if night were a filtration system, sifting away the impurities of each day and returning a distilled, pared light—photons shed of mass. I grind coffee beans and turn on a kettle of water before putting on my jacket and my gumboots. *See you on the flip side,* I say to my empty coffee cup.

To get to the Quonset where Comet's halter and vet supplies are, I walk past old lilac bushes and copses of willows. The yard was landscaped when we bought the place and it's one of the things that made me want to buy it. The apple trees and flowerbeds all follow the natural curve and slope of the ground. The yard has an expansiveness to it. When I look back at the farmhouse, it makes me think of Andrew Wyeth's painting *Christina's World.* Except that I am not as far away from the house as Christina was in the painting, and we've painted our old farmhouse a pale yellow with orange trim. A few years ago, Wayne installed an underground watering system, and we've attached the hoses that lead to Comet's corral to the faucet next to the vegetable garden, the one nearest the Quonset— *Righty-tighty, lefty-loosey,* I say to myself to make sure I've turned the tap in the right direction.

The door of the metal shed squeaks on its hinges and bangs shut behind me. I wonder if Comet has heard this and if he is glad someone's come or if it has put him on edge. I've set up the supplies on an old table. Before Wayne left, he and Brian constructed a small shelter at the other end of the building, the two metal doors pulled open so Comet could come in from the corrals. I fill the oral syringe with the liquid antibiotics, grab the bottle of Fura-Zone, the jar of Swat, and put a few horse treats in my pocket. I think of my neighbour Joyce, who trains horses and says, "I don't do treats." I will do whatever it takes to get Comet to like me. I can hear Wayne saying, "It's not a question of *like*. You can love a horse but it doesn't make a heck of a lot of difference to them. That's not what they're looking for; they're looking for good solid direction, consistency."

I walk out to the pen with as much resolve and determination as I can muster—*Comet, you are going to let me put the syringe in your mouth. You are going to let me halter you and hose you for twenty minutes.* I think of something else Wayne says when trying to support the argument that horses don't mind doing things for us: "They're big. If they didn't want to do what you asked them to, they'd kick your lights out."

I carry my cellphone in my pocket so I can time myself. Whatever happens, it won't be because I haven't done exactly what the vet has instructed. Twenty minutes twice a day.

Comet is standing at the far end of the pen. He is looking at me. I might be imagining it, but he looks pathetic. Gone seems the quickness of his movements, the light in his eyes. His wound gapes as if an entity has taken over, assumed control. A friendly mare called Bailey and a young pinto gelding named Ronnie were held back from the other spares who were sent to the Hutterites, the idea being that they'd be company for Comet, even though they'd have to stay on the other side of the fence. Comet can't be in direct contact with other horses, the reason as clear as the gash in his flesh—they might start pushing each other around. Comet is contained in a small pen to discourage even his own movement. The sight of his containment, of his big scarlet wound that looks like a good part of him is missing, makes me panic—what if he doesn't survive?

"Hey Comet," I say and walk up slowly. It's no problem getting the halter on him—I mean, let's be serious, the horse is wounded, and besides, I've spent a few weeks on the trail every summer for the past seven years. If I can't put a halter on by now, then I truly am a loser.

My first year on the trail I rode Hazel. Poor Hazel, the indecencies she's had to suffer at the hands of novices like me. I remember what a big deal it was to get the bit in and out of a horse's mouth. I was terrified I'd hurt the horse. That first year, so anxious to get the bridle out of Hazel's mouth at the end of the day, I slipped it off with the reins still tied to a tree. Hazel reared her head up in alarm and for sure the bit would have jarred her teeth. I couldn't sleep all that night, the scene playing over and over in my head. The next year, I graduated to Spunky, who had more energy than Hazel and was more suited to my build, both of us finer-boned.

"You look good on that horse," Wayne would say.

A few years after that, needing Spunky for other guests, I started to ride Bucky, a gelding used mostly as a pack horse because he was good at it, but also because he had a nervous streak that made him inconsistent. Bucky and I got along. We were of the same nature. I felt we understood each other.

I lead Comet to the inside pen, where the water hose awaits. He follows easily. I tie him to the fence, stick the syringe into the side of his mouth, and for a moment forget that he is wounded. The power with which he jerks his whole body backward, tossing his head into the air, feels absolute. My heart races. A man's horse. I think of phoning Emilie, but how lame is that. I can't give up that fast. I loosen the rope and tie it to a lower rung of the corral so his head is down. I push the syringe into his mouth again and squeeze the plunger as he tries to rear his head but can't, the fence board shuddering on its nails. Some of the antibiotic dribbles back out of Comet's mouth. I think again of Joyce, who said that in the end, the most important thing would be the rinsing of his shoulder. I loosen the rope so Comet can move his head freely, and then I turn on the hose, feeling the water first to make sure the sun hasn't made it too warm. I turn the nozzle toward Comet's wound, the water touches the open flesh and Comet jumps to the side, flinches, and then holds still.

As I spray his shoulder, the water unhooks ragged flesh, some of it crusty with pus, some of it stuck to the stitches and looking like crushed bumblebees. There is blood on Comet's nose so I know he's been biting at his wound.

"The stitches likely won't stay," the vet had said, and that's where the blood, a watery glaze, is running out from, where the stitches have closed the deepest part of the wound. I focus my spraying there.

"It activates the healing process," the vet had told me, "and it keeps the wound clean."

I keep pulling my cellphone out and checking the time. At twenty minutes exactly, I stop. It's like a recipe. Twenty minutes is what it seems to take for the flesh and scabbed skin to soften and start to peel away, for the bits of straw to loosen and fall, the wound opening back to raw. "Like pizza with the cheese pulled off," is how Brian put it.

Almost immediately, flies begin to land on the open gash. That is what the Swat is for. It's pink as Pepto-Bismol but with the consistency of hard butter, and I apply it all around the edges of the wound. It feels like I am finger-painting, and every now and then I gingerly press down on the very edge of the hide that opens into the wound just to feel how thick a horse-hide is. It is at least a quarter of an inch, the curb of it surrounding the wound as though framing an abstract painting. I squirt the anti-infectant Fura-Zone—the colour of furniture varnish—directly on the wound. I hope Comet lives.

I untie him, take off his halter and walk into the Quonset, but he doesn't follow. I pour some oats into a basin and stand in the makeshift shelter but the horse refuses to come near, so I bring it out to him. Each day, morning and night, I will pull the basin closer and closer to the shelter. Each day, morning and night, we will learn the routine of his wound.

FOURTEEN

Directions

Wayne and I both grew up in northeastern BC. Our childhood homes as well as our adult ones were never much more than an hour's drive apart.

When Wayne was twenty-one, a skidder rolled on top of him, and he spent a few months in the Dawson Creek hospital; it was around the same time that I was a candystriper at the same facility. In 1994, we both attended the Ben Heppner concert at Unchagah Hall. At least once, we both donated pieces to the local art auction. But if we met at any of those times, neither of us can remember.

In 1984, when Wayne embarked on a three-month horse trip into BC's northern Rockies with his girl-friend Carol-Anne, crossing rivers, travelling through meadows, up and over mountains, beginning to see more clearly the difference between the landscape he was travelling through and the clear-cuts he'd helped to create, I had been married for four years and was pregnant with my second child.

When the Mount Le Moray area near Hasler Flats, the place where Wayne had grown up, was under threat of logging, Wayne, along with his partner and other concerned citizens, formed the Chetwynd Environmental Society. Together they began a campaign to protect the last unroaded watershed of any size in the Dawson Creek timber supply area.

"Wayne, it can never be done," some said. "They've already laid out where the roads and cut blocks will be. That valley is a goner."

That was circa 1990. My younger child would soon be starting school.

With an eye on some spare time ahead, I decided to get serious with my lifelong interest in art. In the fall of 1991, I enrolled in the visual arts program at Northern Lights College.

"Back to school?" my mom said. "How will that work?"

The Chetwynd Environmental Society held public meetings, gave slide shows, attended trade shows, signed up hundreds of people as park supporters. My young family must have attended some of those trade shows, but at that time, the focus would have been on my children as they roamed the booths for giveaway stickers and balloons.

It was through the campaign to create a provincial park that the land and resource management planning began, a process that, according to Wayne, took strong negotiation skills. "You had to have a goal in mind," he says, "and you couldn't take no for an answer."

Wayne's bargaining skills were honed from logging for his father. "It required a high level of firmness to get my paycheque signed," Wayne says. "If you could get the old man to take a buck from his pocket, it was squeaking all the way."

In 1992, once the campaign to protect the Mount Le Moray area (which would become the Pine Le Moray Provincial Park) had moved into the planning process, Wayne turned his attention to the northern Rockies, the Muskwa–Kechika.

It was the same year I completed my associate of arts degree. It was also the year I was selected to attend the BC Festival of the Arts as both a visual artist and a writer. It had taken years for me to believe that my passions were worth pursuing. I started a spreadsheet plotting out how I might complete a graduate degree.

In 1998, through a land and resource management plan (LRMP), the Muskwa–Kechika Management Area was established. In his address announcing the creation and protection of the Muskwa–Kechika, New Democratic Party Premier Glen Clark announced: "Perhaps no single land-use decision anywhere has moved sustainability forward so dramatically through conservation, resource development and cooperative management ... In turn, we challenge the rest of the world to follow our example."

By 1998, my children had become teenagers. They were getting their driver's licences, they were falling in and out of love, they were thinking about what they would like to do with their lives. I could see they had already moved beyond the home they'd grown up in. By then I had turned my creative attention away from visual art, toward writing.

In 2001, the Muskwa–Kechika Management Area was expanded by way of the Mackenzie Land and Resource Management Plan, bringing the total area to 6.4 million hectares—one of the largest, most diverse wilderness areas in North America.

For Wayne, those early days at the LRMP tables were charged and uncertain. There was no guarantee that after all of their work the government would approve their recommendations.

"We used to tape the meetings so the secretary could transcribe them," Wayne says. "I'd listen to those tapes on my way to the next meeting. You gotta love that stuff to do that."

What he loved most was the Muskwa–Kechika. When I first met him, he said it was only when he was in the M–K that he felt at home. "When I'm not there," he said, "I'm just treading water."

As my son left for school in Vancouver, and my daughter soon followed, I cherished with a fierce attention the times when everyone was home and sleeping under the same roof. As those times grew rarer, it was my writing that kept me afloat.

FIFTEEN

Horseshoe

A horseshoe isn't a natural part of the horse, but mountains are a place where horses don't naturally go. In the mountains, horseshoes are necessary.

The horseshoe is aerodynamic, shaped so that its front edge banks toward the direction of travel, its bevelled curve cutting the air as sleekly as the starship *Enterprise* slicing through interstellar space.

When I swing a horseshoe in my hand, it reminds my body of gravity, of the comfort of the earth's metal. The horseshoe is a U, it's a C, it's a sickle of moon and shines best when nailed to the hoof of a horse whose movement polishes it against the surface of the earth.

The shoe is the interface between the horse and the earth—the horse transfers its flex and muscle through the shoe onto the moss and boulders, and the ground transfers the qualities of the moss and boulders through the shoe to the flex and muscle of the horse. On the underside, the shoe becomes scored—by rocks, flakes of metal shaving off in travel, tiny sparks snapping when the shoe flints a boulder—thinning over time like a wedding ring. Tony (short for Antoinette), one of the mares on Wayne's pack string, has a slightly heavy-to-the-left step so her shoe is thinner on the left edge. If a shoe is put on so that the metal of the shoe extends even a hair's breadth beyond the hoof, a thin raised rim will occur where the bottom of the shoe, hammered by the ground with every step, and without a hoof to stop it, pounds upward a thin ridge or lip, as if it's been squeezed like a wax seal.

Eventually, though, the hoof grows beyond the shoe, and the shoe no longer sits firmly on the hoof. The shoe starts to unseat. Sometimes the heads of the nails that fasten the shoe to the hoof pestle off from constant grinding against the earth, and without the nail heads, the shoe loosens, creating a thin crack between shoe and hoof. Rocks or sticks catch in the small gap and slowly the shoe is pried away. The material most likely to unseat a shoe is mud, just like gumbo sucks my gumboots off. A horseshoe falls off the hoof of a horse because it is an inanimate object mated to something alive.

Being on the trail in the mountains with a string of horses means that if a horseshoe comes off, it has to go back on right away. It's a big deal when a horse loses a shoe on the trail. If someone spots a horseshoe sunk like a cookie cutter in the mud or hears the ping of metal on stone, it is the one time they will be applauded for getting off their horse mid-ride. That shoe will be their lucky charm, the toy inside the crackerjack box, their Cinderella slipper. They will be complimented on being alert (also having common sense—proof they don't think horseshoes appear out of nowhere, are dispensable—and how would you feel if your hiking boot came off and someone saw it but trotted on by?).

When a horse has lost a shoe, someone has to help Wayne put the shoe back on. Their job will be to retrieve the tools from wherever Wayne tosses them and to predict as best they can the tool he will need next and have it at the ready, while never losing sight of the fact that their stooped head is in the path of the flying horse hoof nippers. Here is the general order of things:

1. Wayne will take a hoof knife and clean the hoof of dirt and pebbles. He will also look for any injuries.
2. He will then trim the ends of the hoof. With the big nippers, he will clip away any excess hoof. The nippers cut through the hoof as silently as a knife carving through a rind of cantaloupe.
3. With the rasp, he will even out the bottom of the hoof, shreds of hoof grating off white and thick as soap shavings.
4. Wayne will then take the horseshoe and place it on the underside of the hoof, testing to see if it sits flat as a plate on a table. If not, he will hammer the shoe on a rock until it does.
5. Then Wayne will place the fitted shoe on the hoof, take the hammer and pound each nail (eight holes,

eight nails) at an angle so each nail exits the top of the hoof at the angle of the sun's rays in December. The nails are, like the shoe, bevelled so they naturally exit the upper side and veer toward the outside of the hoof.

6. When the nail comes through, Wayne's assistant will take the small blue nippers and clip the sharp ends of the nail off to a square. The assistant will pick up the butt ends of the nail and pocket them so they don't lodge in a horse's hoof.

7. Wayne will then rasp underneath the cut ends of the nipped nail to prevent the hoof from splitting when the nail is bent over.

8. Next, the assistant hands over the clinch block, which Wayne will brace against the cut off end of the nail.

9. Wayne will hammer the nail against the block, starting to bend the nail down against the hoof and setting the shoe solidly in place.

10. With the clincher, he'll finish bending the nail down flush against the hoof.

11. Shoeing a horse on the trail is a challenge. If part of the hoof exceeds the edge of the horseshoe at the end of the process, Wayne will take the big nippers and nip the hoof flush to the shoe.

12. Finally, Wayne will take the rasp and smooth the edge of the hoof against the edge of the shoe. Not only will it look pretty, but it will keep things from catching on any rough edges (which could put the horse back to where it started, that is, missing a shoe, and that's a bad refrain).

When I'm back home, headed to Emilie's for a visit or out to weed the garden, I will find the butt ends of horseshoe nails in my pocket, metal castings that are so sleek and shiny, so sharp—in contrast to the grains of dust and sugar sucked by dew into a crust that clings to the inside seams of my pocket or the string of leather, stiffened by salt and grit, that I keep in my pocket for practising knots—that the metal, with its nature to transfer rather than absorb, seems wide awake and always at the ready, just like the body's senses.

I like to think of myself this way—that just as a horseshoe is the interface between the horse's hoof and the earth, my senses are the interface between my body and the material world. The material world, with its moss and boulders, exerts itself on my senses and my senses transfer those qualities to my body—*How green and lush the moss is!* And in the same way the horse's hoof is protected by its shoe, my body is protected by my senses—*Look out for that slippery rock!* Here's to the horseshoe! Here's to my bright and silvery senses clinched to my body, transferring the shape of the birch leaves, the sound of horses as they move through the buckbrush and pine, the *sshh* of their hides against the leaves like rain coming in from the north, horseshoes glinting as they go.

Wayne, Chancey and I relax in the alpine.

SIXTEEN

Oh, How You Fit Me

Never have I put my body beside a man's and had it fit so well. Bespoke. Your arm under the crook of my neck can be there for hours and still my neck is not sore. You turn toward the back of me; I turn toward the back of you. I am home. I love that you are patient and calm and don't mind if I drink though you haven't touched a drop in nearly twenty years. I have autonomy with you—we both go where we want to go when we want to go there. Tricky thing is I don't get to go where I want very often. But still. I love watching your profile when you sit at your computer. Because you are lean from packing horses and walking up mountain passes and then back down, all summer long, the bones of your body jut out. Maybe because of this, you look even taller than you are already; when I hold you, the blades of your shoulders are like climbing grips or handlebars on a midway ride. Even the bones in your fingers are chiselled. When a mosquito lands on your arm, you lift your finger with such calm assurance the insect doesn't know to move. You are deadly rational. When you're sitting in the kitchen chair putting a battery into your headlamp, glasses pushed down the bridge of your nose, your moustache white, I think of Geppetto, but when you're in the mountains with your red-checked neckerchief and cowboy hat, then I think of Indiana Jones. Sometimes, late at night when you've got your headlamp on because we're in bed and I've been trying to sleep, I watch you read about people who have been thrust into extreme situations—Scott's failed return from the South Pole, or the more exuberant Shackleton, your books piled on your bedside table, precariously, all non-fiction, all things explorational, geological, paleontological—some nights I look at you and think, *How did this man come to be with me?*

SEVENTEEN

Glassing for Poodles

How close do you have to be to a bear to count it as a sighting? Does a bear viewed through binoculars as it heads up a mountain pass count? Or does its breath have to fog the lens so you know yourself as prey and have an out-of-body experience as you pull the bear banger? At some point, an animal through binoculars is no more than an abstract statistic. At some point you have to tell yourself you are looking at a bear. What some say is a sheep on a ridge near the top of a pass on the other side of the valley could be, as someone once told me, a poodle for all they could tell.

Of all the things people take on the trail, one of the most coveted seems to be binoculars—oh, for the finely ground lens, the graphite mould—as though binoculars tucked into a saddlebag were a symbol of humankind's eternal yearning, always reaching beyond our grasp.

A few years ago I attended a writing colony at St. Peter's Abbey in Muenster, Saskatchewan. While there, I experienced a chickadee landing in the palm of my hand. The monks, with their patience and peanuts, had habituated the birds to feed from their hands. A chickadee in your hand is amazing—the way the bird darts into your palm, a clean and muscled weightlessness, the tips of the beak spearing the halved nuts, then the body lifting with a purr of wing takes me a bit outside of myself. The first time one landed, I lurched. But that's what I kept wanting, that ping of unexpectedness. So I braced myself again and again, wanting to feel the whir of something wild.

In *Vis à Vis: Field Notes on Poetry and Wilderness*, Don McKay says there is "the sudden angle of perception, the phenomenal surprise which constitutes the sharpened moments of *haiku* and imagism ... we encounter the momentary circumvention of the mind's categories to glimpse some thing's autonomy—its rawness, its *duende,* its alien being."

In Tim Lilburn's *Living in the World as if It Were Home*, he writes of a deer who appears to know Tim is watching him. The deer returns the gaze—"Their look seems a bestowal," he writes. "I feel more substantial, less apologetic as a physical thing from having been seen." Lilburn seems to speak to a desire to be himself subsumed, made part of something else. As if to receive the gaze of a non-human animal makes us feel, for a moment, a part of their world, a bit less exposed, self-conscious, which is magical in one way but is, in another, perhaps one more manifestation of our acquisitive soul, our yearning to make everything a part of us or for us to be a part of the other. "The weirdness, unreachability of things, is not abolished by any sudden aberration of intimacy, fluked into being by a deer's look, but is intensified by it. The desire to feel otherness as selfhood, to be the deer seeing ourself, remains." In other words, or at least this is my interpretation, if we feel like a deer, then we are the deer; we are no longer the human.

Binoculars compress distance while keeping a distance. Binoculars provide us with an opportunity to observe a wild animal without it knowing it is being watched. And maybe that is the closest we will ever get to allowing a wild animal to remain itself: being far enough away so that it doesn't know we're there, and is therefore still wild, its behaviour unchanged by us.

Mayfield Lake is the place where Wayne feels at home.

EIGHTEEN

The Way a Wound Heals

Wayne has been gone for ten days. In that time, I've mowed the lawn three times, weeded the garden two, and hosed Comet twenty. Twice a week, after work, I stop in to see my parents. One day I walk in just as my dad is coming out of the bathroom, a cockeyed grin on his face. There is no question that he still knows me and is glad to see me. "Just sit down!" my mother says. "Don't come near here." And both my dad and I move toward the living room as my mom rushes into the bathroom with rubber gloves and disinfectant. It's difficult to see them this way. I'm sure my dad knows he has made some kind of a mess, but he doesn't know how to stop it. And my mom, whose strength and vitality, whose love of travel and adventure, has always been an inspiration, is also starting to show signs of wear. But you can't tell my mom what to do. While my sisters and

I have tried to make casual remarks about home care or other kinds of support, any decision will have to be hers. In the meantime, life for both of my parents feels very trapped.

I've heard from Wayne twice. Because his satellite phone has to be turned off to save batteries, I have to wait for him to call me. I make lists of the things I need or want to tell him—messages from clients, questions I have, the most recent one being, "Where is the temporary electric fencing?" I've decided that Comet needs a better place to live. There's nothing for him to do, nothing to explore. I figure I can put him in the bigger fenced-in area where the hay is stored. I'll put temporary electric fencing around the hay bales so Comet can have the rest of the space, which includes granaries that he can stand beside for shelter and an open area where grass is growing. He can eat grass. It's summer, for god's sake.

Each day I take a picture of Comet's wound, but after ten days, I can't see any improvement, just an ongoing saga of change. The stitches have come undone, just like the vet said they might, and now the wound is bigger than ever. It is its own continent, a land formed by an underlying geology of flesh and muscle. In the upper east is a thick frothy yellow ooze that seems to continually pipe out from beneath the hide, as if it were the mouth of a geyser. Ooze that I hose away and that, almost right away, comes back. Adjacent and to the west is a scape of cracked flesh, reddish and grey like the parched bottom of a riverbed. And to the south is the cavernous territory

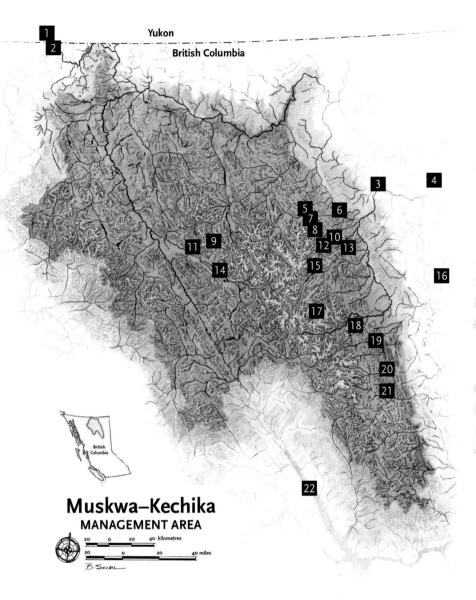

Yukon

British Columbia

British Columbia

Muskwa–Kechika
MANAGEMENT AREA

20 0 20 40 kilometres
20 0 20 40 miles

B. SWAIL

1 Watson Lake	9 Bevin Lake and Pass	16 Prophet River
2 Lower Post	10 Chisca River	17 Gathto Creek
3 Kledo Creek	11 Gataga River	18 Muskwa River
4 Fort Nelson	12 Northern Caribou Range	19 Prophet River Hotsprings
5 Summit Lake Trailhead	13 Tuchodi River	20 Besa River
6 Tetsa River	14 Mayfield Lakes	21 Trimble Lake
7 Twin Lakes	15 Tuchodi Lakes	22 Williston Lake
8 Henry Creek		

A bull moose visits his local watering hole at Mayfield Lake on a misty evening.

Nights can be cold in the alpine. In the distance, artists at the Muskwa–Kechika Camp gather around a fire above Mayfield Lakes and South Gataga River.

I scrub the dishes while the rest of the crew goes in search of Ulla, the missing horse.

The body of Ulla, the pack horse—a speck in an alpine tarn—floats against a backdrop of wind, cloud and valley.

Hazel pauses to graze before the next segment of the trail.

After a major fire in spring 2006, new life bursts from the burn.

Hazel senses that I need a break partway up the trail.

Wayne leads the pack string down the West Toad River area to the Alaska Highway. DONNA KANE

Hobbles don't deter Paint as he crosses an arm of the Muskwa River, following the herd to the next grazing spot.

On a high remote pass, a July snow shower surprises me.

The pack string traverses the grassy hillsides along West Tuchodi Lake.

Break time. The expedition soaks in the beauty of the Northern
Caribou Range.

Who knew the volume of supplies needed for a two-week expedition?

A storybook moment on the trail with blue sky and my friends and family beside the Gataga River, part of the trek from Mayfield Lake to the Tuchodi Lakes.

After Hazel, I build trust with Spunky.

A bull moose struts through the hobbled pack string at the headwaters of the Prophet River.

Wayne and I share a moment at East Tuchodi Lake before I head back to Rolla and Wayne continues on the trail. JERRY PAVIA

A grizzly strides past the pack string.

Hazel and I ferry Chancey, the border collie, across the Gatho River.

Wayne re-shoes Paint after some tough slogging on the trail.

Comet and I in the Northern Caribou Range.

Brian Jungen (left) calms Comet as his injury gets emergency treatment from Dr. Christa Harder (middle) and her assistant Brenda. SCOTT MOORE

Comet, healed. October 2013. DONNA KANE

The upper Gatho River is one of the most spectacular areas in the Muskwa–Kechika and one of the richest in wildlife.

Hazel is alpha of the herd and best friend to many a new rider.

made up of the deepest part of his wound, gullies and ravines, the cut muscles below directing the flow of blood.

Comet's wound is a conversation piece. When people come to visit, they all want to see it, and even if they don't, and if Emilie's around, she will insist, "Have you seen Donna's horse? You have to see it." *Donna's horse.*

I no longer tie Comet to the fence rail when I hose him. It's easier for both of us if I hold the lead rope in one hand and the hose in the other, the water's spray tearing small perforations into a greyish tissue that is forming over the wound, the water entering beneath the tissue and then spurting out other slits in the film. Some days I feel like I'm washing my car, the hose working away at bits of loose flesh like the last bit of gumbo clinging to the mud flaps, clinging and clinging and then off it goes. Sometimes, hosing Comet is the most relaxing part of my day. When he is calm, hosing is a bit like Zen, a practice I fall into, fade in and out of. Comet must feel it too. When we're about ten minutes in, he will heave a big sigh.

A many-plumed moth settles on a book.

NINETEEN

The Gaze

O h, bliss of *tiny* creatures," wrote Rilke (in "The Eighth Elegy") "that remain / for ever in the womb that brought them forth!" After twisting a corner of a tissue into a makeshift rope, I dunk the tip of it into my wineglass and wait for the moth that has flown into my drink to grab on. The moth swims valiantly but badly, its scales slipping off, leaving a silvery wake, a slick that shines as if lit by the moon, which strikes me as doubly tragic because the bedside lamp probably cast its glow on the wine's surface, making the Merlot seem a moon to traverse by, and now the flotsam of the moth's wings are adding to the overall sheen. When the moth clasps the rope, I hoist the insect up and set it on the window ledge. I wait for the moth to emerge from the folds of the Kleenex, stripped to its fretwork, joints bristle-bright, antennae waving as if feverish to know what is left of its body.

In his elegy, Rilke wrote, "We alone see [death]; the free animal / has its decease perpetually behind it ..." How could Rilke have known? I examine the moth. The moth's focus seems unfazed as it cripples along the ledge, carrying onward toward who knows where. It would be easy to imagine the moth as unaffected by its fate. But anything from a certain distance tends to take on an indifferent air. When an astronaut takes a picture of Earth from outer space, the planet looks like a blown-glass bauble, a unified singular object. I hardly ever think of myself as part of it. At such a distance, it seems I don't exist. But I must be there, in some of those photos.

If I look at a tiny grey moth resting with its wings fully opened, flattened against a window frame or upside down on a wall, it appears as a shred of wasp nest, a flake of hammered silver. But if I take my glasses off and peer with my nearsighted eyes, the moth becomes startlingly clear. I can see the lacework of the moth's wings, a brindled filigree like the tail feathers of a grouse, a striped fan of brown and white trimmed in copper. I can see the moth's face, two bright eyes like minuscule beads of oil on a head small as a grain of sand. I can see the moth's antennae witching the air I breathe. I have no way of knowing if the moth is staring at me, but that's how it feels, that an exchange has been made.

When a "dumb brute's calmly / raising its head to look us through and through," says Rilke, we see the reflection of "the free and open," an outward gaze unburdened by "consciousness such as we have." I have stared hard at these tiny moths. I have tried to see the blissful ignorance that Rilke thought was "so deep within the brute's face." But nothing of such privilege has come. I could never see how the moth was unaware of its existence. I could never see how it was oblivious to its death. Maybe when two different species look at each other, and neither one knows what the other one is thinking, it only feels like "the open."

I have always felt the pleasure of reflection. When I was a child, we had a *World Book Encyclopedia*. I loved the pebbled texture of the faux leather covers and the gold-coloured letters embossed on each spine. My favourite volume was *H*. Inside was a chapter on human anatomy. One of the gilt-edged pages was blank. Overtop that page were several thin sheets of plastic. On each sheet were coloured images of different parts of a man's body—the bones, the internal organs, the circulatory system, the muscles. The images were aligned so that, when each sheet was superimposed over top of the one below, it altered the appearance of the man. Each sheet built upon the last until the man was made whole. It impressed upon me at a very young age that I would never get to see the inside of my own body, my own heart and lungs. Even more astonishing was the realization that I would never see my own face as it appeared to others. All I ever saw was my reflection. I would look in the mirror and see my blue eyes, my imperfect nose, my mouth with the tiny scar on the upper lip from the time I got thrown from a tire swing. I would study my features in two dimensions. Using the mirror for direction, I would raise my arm to touch my right cheek and find I'd touched my left one instead. *How strange, I thought, that others see me in ways I cannot.*

Being aware of thinking makes me wonder what it would be like to not think, to turn my gaze, as Rilke suggests, outward into "the open." Yet there is such pleasure in thinking, in being aware, and Rilke must have felt that too. Many believe the *Duino Elegies*, which include "The Eighth Elegy," is one of the greatest poetic works of the twentieth century.

The encyclopedia also had a section on human intelligence. There was a diagram that compared humans to other animals. The images were in black silhouette and each animal was given a standing, a rung on the ladder of cognition. A horse was smarter than a rat. A pig was smarter than a horse. Humans were at the top. It didn't occur to me then that the intelligence of a pig or a horse or a rat was determined by how closely its behaviour matched ours.

Bats navigate the dark by sound. A wheatear flies from Alaska to Africa, yet we're still not sure what guides it. I am limited by my own particular way of thinking, my own particular senses. Rilke's thinking goes along these lines too. He suggests that our way is unchangeably distinct from that of all other animals, and he writes that it is our fate, "being opposite, / and nothing else, and always opposite." But wouldn't that be the fate of non-human animals as well?

My cat puts his paw on my face when he's hungry. He opens doors with levered handles. *How intelligent,* I think, as if these sorts of acts prove his cognition while everything else he does in a day, things I can't understand, do not. Maybe Rilke intended the irony at the heart of "The Eighth Elegy." Perhaps he meant for me to catch the contradiction in claiming, on the one hand, that humans can't know beyond their own perceptions, their own way of thinking, and then, on the other, to claim we can know what goes on in the brains of non-human animals.

There was one time when a moth fell into my glass and wouldn't accept the tissue I offered. I had to use my fingers. Feeling the moth's body, equal to the thickness of embroidery thread, pinched between my thumb and forefinger, startled me. Recognizing the moth's vulnerability, its thin film of chitin, a hardened protein that protects its heart in the same way my flesh separates my internal organs from the rest of the world, caused me to drop the moth. It landed on top of a bookmark I'd left on the window ledge. One of the moth's wings was crushed beyond repair. I stared at it. The moth looked dead. I picked it up, gingerly, intending to put it in the waste bin but it was as if a small gust of wind blew it from my fingertips. It went back to the bookmark and sat. Each morning and night I'd give it a poke. It would flutter up and then settle back down. It did what it did on the bookmark with its crushed wing and then, at the end of three days, it died.

Its body went from powdered membrane to dust, and no way, I thought, would I look so tidy in death, so gossamer. The moth fades, desiccates, and doesn't leave a stain on my window ledge. Or so it all seems from this distance.

When someone tells me they've transcended thought and experienced pure being, that "openness," I imagine, of Rilke's elegy, I am eager to know how they got there. Some say they meditate. I've tried that, and I confess it makes me cranky. I know it takes work and patience and maybe I haven't tried hard enough.

Some say they stare at an object until the thoughts and words they'd attached to the object disappear. They look until a film of perception unglues and they see beyond the object. I've tried that too, and sometimes my mind goes blank, sometimes I feel calmer, but I have never felt any real enlightenment.

I have had this experience: catching sight of a familiar object in a place where I didn't expect to see it—timothy grass, for example, so common to the paths and fields I walked as a child, appearing in a vase in an art gallery in New York. Or I'll be fumbling with a button or a lock and it won't work the way I expect it to. In those moments, my memories, my old perceptions, are temporarily numbed, anaesthetized, and, for a moment at least, I glimpse these objects with a detached eye. I see the thing, not as if for the first time, but in the way that metaphor works—out of context. The object flares strange but razor bright. If I've ever thought I might be on to something, it's during these moments. But the material world was still present, and my senses, if anything, were more revved up than ever. And when the moment passed, and my feeling of close-to-something-like-an-answer vanished, what I was left with was a reminder of how small I am, how insubstantial—a fleck of something in a universe of countless other flecks, flecks with parts that can't be known by others, parts that can't even be known by me. And yet I can't stop thinking about it. I can't stop wondering what it would be like to break free of myself. But if I could, I would still want to know what I was seeing. I would still want to think about it. I would not want my consciousness to disappear entirely, to have it become invisible to me. No. What I want is to break free, as Rilke said, of "the womb that brought [us] forth" and then, when I've had a good look around, to come back and reflect on it. I would like to go where Rilke went when he wrote the *Duino Elegies*. Some say it was after he heard the voice of an angel. When I read "The Eighth Elegy," I am reading a translation of Rilke's original work. My comprehension of it is yet another kind of translation. I read it even so.

I take a sip of the Merlot, no hint of moth. I look at the tiny creature on the window ledge. It shakes its diminished body, then, with its joints twitching, I watch as it drags its thinned shadow toward—what, a will to survive? Perhaps. Though it looks, just now, a little more like hope.

Horse blankets dry in the sun on a camp day at Heaven's Pass.

TWENTY

Rituals of a Wound

Every day Comet's wound begins to scab over and every day I hose the scab away—think of a marshmallow roasted in the fire just long enough to form a crust that you then pull off, the sticky goo put back in the fire and roasted again. It feels a bit counterproductive—every day the healing that Comet's body undergoes is taken away. But when I compare the wound to the picture I took a few weeks ago, I can see that the flesh is a lighter pink now, also pebbled, less oozy though still raw.

As the days go by, I realize I've come to enjoy the practice of getting up and going out to hose Comet. The fresh exuberance of morning is hard to ignore. When I was a teenager I'd sleep in on the weekends and my dad would always admonish me for missing the best part of the day. *Dad, I now know what you meant.* Even on the worst days, when it's rainy or I haven't slept well, I can feel my body doing little jumps for joy at the aesthetic pleasure of morning, seeing the grass getting greener, the lilacs flowering, the fleece flower, lupines, daisies and columbines getting lusher, everything bursting with life, morning exposing the core of it.

I have established a routine. Out of bed at 6:00 a.m., I slip into whatever work clothes are at hand, go downstairs and put the kettle on to boil, grind the coffee beans and then put on my coat and gumboots, out the door, across the lawn past the lilac trees, down the slope of the yard to the Quonset, hose Comet, Fura-Zone, Swat, then to the farther corrals, ducking under the fence, through the grassy area that leads to where I feed Comet, the repetition of my route packing down my trail around an anthill, through the quack grass, around a wild rose bush to the hay bales.

When my children were little, we had traditions, things we did on birthdays and at Christmastime, rituals I now look back on with nostalgia and longing. As if I became who I was through the rituals I'd learned, and now, having lost those traditions, I feel lost, bewildered.

Many rituals are borne out of necessity. "What works, survives," says Wayne. The practices that prove successful are the ones that continue on into the future. There are many habits turned ritual on the trail and nearly all of them are there to make the work efficient. When we come into camp, there is a certain sequence repeated every day, after we tie up our saddle horses. Our first task is to unpack the pack horses. We put the panniers in a row, the gear in its respective spots—bridles hung on a tree, saddles placed on their backs, stacking one on top of the other. Once the pack horses are unpacked and each one is hobbled and turned loose, we do the same with the saddle horses, each rider doing his or her own. Then the cooking gear is unpacked, someone lights a fire, someone else goes for water, and once the kettle is on the grate and the cook's happy, then and only then do people disperse to put up their tents. This particular sequence is the most efficient way of setting up camp and getting supper started so you have time to enjoy the evening and relax without having to cook in the dark. The repetition becomes a kind of mantra, and it is comforting not only in its familiarity but because it works, it's efficient—saddles off, people fed.

The route I take to see Comet becomes a trail because it gets me to the horse and to the hay bales the quickest. Walking the trail each morning has given rise to a kind of comfort. Wayne will say that in the mountains he likes his trails—they reassure him that he's in the right place, give him something to follow. Most of the time he is following game routes, but sometimes he makes his own way. It's possible that this changes the habits of moose and caribou and bears, animals that might use Wayne's way instead. Particle physics claims that every time we are observed we are changed, and that we change others just by observing them. Perhaps a standard by which to assess the impacts of change, whatever it might be, is to determine whether or not that change alters our own routines, our own efficiencies.

I can see that my interactions with Comet are changing him. When he sees me coming, his ears perk up. He has grown used to the routine, to the treats I offer while I spray water on him, the oats I bring when we're done. And he knows that between the end of rinsing and bringing out the oats, I have to apply ointments and fly repellent to his wound. In the beginning, after I'd finished hosing, I would tie him up to the fence and then go pick up the Fura-Zone and Swat where I'd set them on the ground. Now, when the hosing's done, I take Comet's halter off and leave him standing freely. He stands and waits for me to return with the ointments. Only when they've been applied does he head toward the Quonset and stand inside, waiting in expectation of oats.

And our interactions have changed me. I think of him when I'm not there. I think of the wound and how it feels when I place the palm of my hand against it, the way the heat transfers to my hand and sometimes, also, how it leaves a thin etching of blood. I think of Comet's mane and tail, how it feels to brush the knots away, I think of the places where he likes to be rubbed, places he can't easily reach, the velvet hollow where his back legs meet his belly. My perception of him has changed. I've learned that he can be pushy for attention and a little stubborn. I've learned he can be arrogant and strong, but that he is never as strong as he thinks he is. I talk to him. "Comet, did you know that at the Royal Ascot, if you want to sit in the Royal

Enclosure you have to wear a headpiece big enough to qualify as a hat, not a fascinator? Which means the headpiece has to be bigger than ten centimetres. Your wound is much bigger, but ten centimetres is still pretty big for a glorified barrette. Oh, there is fascination everywhere. Rolla in the summer is a bit of a carnival, have you noticed? People arrive on their way to the mountains and people arrive on their way back down and lots of them want to look at you, and when Wayne calls, he always asks how we are."

When people stop on their way up, I give them letters for Wayne with pictures of Comet's wound. When the guests return, they bring notes back. Last week, in a bag of Wayne's laundry, I found a thick curl of birch bark. With a felt marker, Wayne had drawn a heart with an arrow through it, and inside the heart, he'd written our initials.

I spend a camp day hiking above the Gatho River.

TWENTY-ONE

Hiking to the Top of the Ridge

I think again of how a footprint communicates the way thought and language do, that a single track or footprint is like the subject of a sentence, but to be a complete sentence, for thought to emerge, you need action, a predicate. For a predicate, for meaning to emerge, one foot has to make contact twice. There has to be movement.

Sometimes I like to go one step further—to think of my body as the subject and my mind as its predicate. Together we make a sentence where meaning emerges. But when my body and my mind are both in action, then we're really cooking with gas.

Walking has always been one of my greatest pleasures, and not just on the trail, though I feel the pleasure of it there most keenly—to be on my own, free of the demands of the pack string; a camp day on which, if the weather is good, I climb up through the buckbrush where Bucky gets squirrelly, prepared to bolt, because he can't see over the briars, up to where the vegetation grows thin and the shale bares itself, scrambling up a scree slope where no horse would ever go and where it's best if I don't look down, to the ridge where I walk along, zigzagging as I make my way steadily higher, amazed at how much distance I gain in ascension, how the camp's blue overhead tarp dissolves into the trees, the place I've been an Alka-Seltzer tablet fizzing away, all the details, the grit of the day, and what I have is panorama, a point where I can see over every mountain range, and the view gives rise to an ache in my belly.

To walk is to act on an insatiable hunger for more, and when I stand at the top of a mountain I can see so much more. I can see places I have never been and also places I have—there's the lake, the Gataga, the strip of burned trees, the landscape loosening its limbs with each distinction: the sandbar, the marsh, the path to the creek, each part phosphorescing like lamps turning on, wick by wick, inside me.

They say that charting the Milky Way is like mapping a crowded city from within its midst. If we could travel outside of it, then we'd see the place more clearly. I've tried to picture the Earth as though I weren't on it, to imagine the spin and tilt of an object parted, but I could never detach from my body's weight. I'd get as far as imagining myself looking down—always looking down, never up, which may have something to do with my relationship with gravity. But even if I get to the imagined *up there*, I can't break free of Earth's tether. I can't get my feet off the ground, outside of its midst and frame of reference, from the place where thought takes shape and matters. Sometimes I think I walk to escape myself. I can imagine walking so fast I break free of my body. I think that I write for the same reason.

Wayne leads the pack string safely across Upper Tuchodi River.

TWENTY-TWO

Wilderness

One year I rode with Wayne's pack string for the first two legs of the expedition, starting at the abandoned Summit Lake Lodge at Mile 392 of the Alaska Highway. Into the hills we went, nine riders and twenty horses full of piss and vinegar after nine months of rest. We followed a game trail along the North Tetsa River, where bears pawed up the roots of hedysarum and a harlequin duck swam in the rocky pool as we crossed the swift-moving river.

It was spring, the landscape awash in anemone and bluebells, in the songs of ruby-crowned kinglets, warblers and sparrows. We crossed the North Tetsa, riding up a pass and then down, then up again, along a muddy and root-snarled trail to the plateau of Twin Lakes, then down to where the weather was active, going from cloud to rain to sun to wind, as if in love with its possibilities and restless for each, to Henry

Creek—where our dog paced an ice ledge on the bank before plunging in for the swim and I thought she would drown, her body fighting the current, her eyes never once leaving the sight of Wayne, my eyes never leaving the sight of her, until she reached the opposite shore, and Wayne never looking back, the whole time confident she'd make it—up into a wide plateau in the subalpine where a herd of mountain caribou came bounding toward us, and we stopped the pack string and watched them come. They may never have seen such large strange objects before. They ran toward us to see what we were about and the pack horses ran toward them, their panniers filled with rice and turnips and coffee jostling on their backs, the riders pulling out their cameras, the dog told to sit, all of us held in a moment of interspecies curiosity, checking each other out, before the pack string moved on to the Chisca River area where the treeline stopped and the sheer limestone mountains rose so high I thought of Everest—a broad band of impenetrable brown and grey—with the sun getting low so that, behind one of the cliffs it threw a mountain shadow against the sky, the shape of the rock reflecting in the dust in the air. It is said that on nights when it is very dark, and the sky is clear, the shadow of the Earth can be seen just like this, its curve blocking the light of the sun whose rays reflect off the interstellar dust around our planet's cut-out. I watched the mountain's reflection as I rode along, the ground a wet seep from a small underground spring where the lupines flourished and smelled like honey.

When we reached the alpine on the Northern Caribou Range, it was cloudless and warm, and we stopped to sit on the slope with the forget-me-nots and moss campion, and camped for the night. Margison Creek and the thin veins of snow in the mountain crevasses were visible from the door of our tent. The next morning we descended into the broad Tuchodi River Valley, travelling upriver, crossing side channels to East Tuchodi Lake. From there, we crossed the Tuchodi River—glacial flour colouring the water pewter, giving it an opacity, a body, the current a broad rippling muscle riding the river's spine, its shape thick enough for its waves to cast shadows on the water—I carried the dog on the horse, then led the horse up a steep incline before descending to Gathto Creek, where we camped, and from where I walked to the top of a ridge, found the bleached skull of a fox, held it in my hands while the sound of horse bells rose from the valley.

Before Kluachesi Lake, the river crossing was rough and Brian was tossed into the chuck, had to scramble up the bank. We travelled back down to Tuchodi Lake, and the next day a jet boat took me and the rest of the outgoing crew down the Muskwa River to Kledo Creek just north of Fort Nelson, where I got in my truck to drive back to Rolla.

Not once in the twenty-five days and roughly two hundred miles we'd travelled had I seen another human being other than the people I was with. The cumulus clouds formed, cast shadows then disappeared and the sun came out and glanced off the mountain cliffs and more clouds moved in and it rained and the slopes turned a sheen of iridescent green and night fell and day came and then dusk. Sometimes I would feel an intense rush of freedom, a sense that I was in a world that existed without me— mountain peaks that cloned themselves plate after plate, the coulees of snow that melted then spilled over broad smooth rocks forming gelatinous waves falling into the inception of creeks that threaded through meadows of hellebore and anemones, the world's beauty going on without any human intervention. A world for which I was not responsible.

"You can find wilderness anywhere," the poet Tim Lilburn once told me while sitting in a café in Victoria, giving a small shrug toward the window. "You can go to Mount Doug and find wilderness." It was raining and the café windowpane was steamed up. I looked across the street at the Belfry Theatre. A few miles beyond that, lost in the mist, was Mount Douglas. I could have walked to it from where we sat dunking our tea bags made out of a silken material of such quality I probably didn't own a shirt that nice, and inside that chi-chi fabric were crushed flowers, bits of stems and petals.

A few summers ago, poet Simon Armitage walked the Pennine Way from Kirk Yetholm, on the other side of the Scottish border, to Edale in Derbyshire, a span of roughly two hundred and sixty miles. In his wonderful account of that journey, *Walking Home,* he refers to the Pennine Way as wilderness. *But wait a minute,* I thought when I read it, *there were signs along the trail, and fences to keep in sheep and cows, and every night*

he reached a village where he could buy toothpaste and
where pubs pulled their taps of brew while he read poetry
to the locals and where he slept on a mattress in houses
equipped with plumbing and heat and where every day, at
some point on the trail, he would meet or be accompanied
by someone he didn't know, a trail that could be nearly
always traversed by an ATV, *a trail he was often delivered*
to each morning by car. Maybe I was being unfair, but I
felt proprietary about the idea of wilderness, as if I had
exclusive rights to it. Which was silly, and more than a
little ironic.

American activist Robert Marshall said wilderness
is "sufficiently spacious that a person in crossing it
must have the experience of sleeping out." The 1964
US Wilderness Act states that wilderness is "where
man himself is a visitor who does not remain."

Does it matter if we use the word *wilder-*
ness to describe both the Pennine Way and the
Muskwa–Kechika?

"Well, for sure there is a danger," Wayne will say.
"You don't want to get those things confused. If you
can say that a developed agricultural landscape or a
formally industrial landscape that's now abandoned is
wilderness, then you have thrown the doors wide open
for exploitation. If the word *wilderness* can be used for
areas where there has been development, we lose the
standard for what should be protected."

Don McKay, in *Vis à Vis: Field Notes on Poetry and*
Wilderness, wrote that "by 'wilderness' I want to mean,
not just a set of endangered spaces, but the capacity of
all things to elude the mind's appropriations." Which

is what Tim Lilburn was likely getting at too—"You can find wilderness in a teakettle" was something else he said.

Would the word *wildness* be more appropriate when describing metaphysical states of unknowability? Perhaps, but *wilderness* has more heft, somehow feels as though it has more to sink our imagination into. Is it because the word *wildness* has remained an abstract, like beauty or greed, and because, like those concepts, wildness has no mass?

Wilderness, on the other hand, is used by some to describe both the metaphysical quality of an object (its unknowability) and the physical thing itself—the Muskwa–Kechika, the Pennine Way. In its definition of the word, the *Canadian Oxford Dictionary* uses adjectives like "uncultivated" and "uninhabited." Most often, wilderness is described as a physical place; unlike wildness, it has weight and mass. While concepts like wildness and beauty retain their abstraction, continue to reign in the heavens of our mind, wilderness seems to have fallen with a thump to Earth.

If this is true, then it makes our preference for the word *wilderness* when describing the capacity of things to "elude the mind's appropriations" a bit ironic. But it is also how metaphor works. The word *wilderness* is easier for us to get a handle on because it is easier for us to sense. We can hold bits of it in our hands, feel its weight and shape. *Wilderness*, unlike *wildness*, is, quite literally, easier for us to grasp, and so we use the label to describe that which is beyond our grasp.

The Muskwa–Kechika Advisory Board spent many years trying to reach a consensus on how to define *wilderness*.

If the physical places we name as wilderness are themselves mutable, sometimes going from a large landscape with an undisturbed-by-humans ecosystem to a few wooded acres behind someone's house, does it matter? For those who are in the business of protecting wilderness areas, the answer seems to be yes. In the battle to keep the objects or places that wilderness names intact, their qualities must also remain the same.

But is the Muskwa–Kechika really wild? After all, by its very protection it is a product of human intervention. And if people like Wayne take their pack strings through it, churning their way over the trails, is the ecosystem still intact? Wayne will say the changes made to wilderness by his travelling through it are ephemeral. A few years ago, a couple from Argentina followed Wayne's route and later asked if he ever lit campfires because they often couldn't find the places he'd camped.

For now, the concept of the Muskwa–Kechika seems to remain unchanged. It still possesses the qualities of unroaded valleys and undammed rivers and many unnamed mountains, a place with few mapped routes, where bears and caribou are not habituated to humans, a place where you can ride along a cliff at dusk and hear nothing except the squeak of your saddle—no roar of a gas plant, no vehicles driving by, no hum of a fridge or furnace kicking in.

A place where my thoughts seem to echo that silence, reminding me that I need quiet in order to think.

"Did you feel that?" I say to Wayne when we arrive at camp.

"Feel what?"

"The silence."

I want to tell him that the silence I felt along the cliff was filled with reverberations, a palpable awareness, as if the rocks, the trees, the stream were tremoring with a sense of consciousness. I want to say that maybe, just as photons need an object to reflect on in order to turn into light, or gravity requires objects of mass in order to be measured, maybe consciousness is its own kind of force, something that requires an object to reflect on in order to turn into thought. I know what Wayne would say: "That's a bit too woo-wooey for me." And maybe it is. But how extraordinary that we still don't know for certain what consciousness is, how, like gravity, we are deeply aware of its presence, but not of its source. Its wildness remains. The very thing that makes us aware eludes "the mind's appropriations."

There is beauty in wilderness—beauty in its physical manifestations and beauty in its capacity to elude us. James Joyce wrote, in *A Portrait of the Artist as a Young Man*, "The object of the artist is the creation of the beautiful. What the beautiful is is another question." I love this sentence because it serves as both a question and an answer. When I first read the sentence, I take it as a question—what is the beautiful? But when I read it again, it answers the question—the beautiful is another question—there is beauty in the things we can't know, in things that escape the mind's appropriations. Sitting in the alpine on the Caribou Range, or travelling through a silence echoing off the cliff as we near the Prophet River restores me, as though the world were going on without me, bringing me to a place still alive with its own possibilities. Ecologist Aldo Leopold said wilderness "should be big enough to absorb a two-week pack trip." I think wilderness is a place that has not been appropriated by us, either physically or ontologically, a place that retains its beauty because it escapes us.

Mayfield Lake: just another day in paradise.

TWENTY-THREE

Sally

Once upon a time there was a gal named Tessa who sold her horse, Sally, to a fellow named Trevor, to pay for a trip. Trevor, a generous soul, told Tessa that, even though he now owned Sally she should still think of the horse as hers and ride her anytime. Trevor kept Sally, a sorrel mare with a white blaze and a brown mane and tail flecked with strands that glittered in the sun like spun gold, at Emilie's. A few times, on trips home, Tessa would go to Emilie's to ride her horse. But life got busy, things changed, and she stopped coming. Trevor rode Sally once. Like Tessa's father, Trevor sometimes drank too much beer, but unlike Tessa's father, who used to lead Sally to Tessa's trampoline, get on the trampoline and, on an up-bounce, land on Sally's back and gallop her as fast as she'd go across the field, Trevor lacked the experience or maybe the coordination, or both, and fell off. His career as a rider ended. Trevor quit paying board fees and Emilie quit thinking of Sally as Trevor's horse.

Once or twice each summer, Emilie and I will go riding and I'll ride Sally. She's fine-boned, quiet but easily spooked; perhaps the trampoline trick is partly to blame. After our rides, Emilie will always say that I should buy her, that Sally needs someone who understands her, but by the end of the day, Emilie will decide she's not ready to part with Sally, and I'll laugh and say that's okay, I've got my eye on an Italian bicycle and the Vancouver seawall.

This morning I wake up to go riding with Emilie, and no one else is in the house. I can count the number of days on one hand when I've been alone this summer. Many of the guests who come and go have become friends—not just with Wayne and me, but with the entire Rolla community. They stay for the social atmosphere, the impromptu parties and the conversations that go late into the night. In the morning, I'll lie in bed and listen to the voices downstairs, count the number of times the coffee grinder turns on, the number of times the front door opens and shuts. I'll hear the car doors slam and look out the window at the vehicles as they drive in and out, at the lawn I keep mowed and the flowers, which have been spectacular this year. Some might note the weeds but I've given up on the notion of weeding, in part because I'm so short of time and also because the flowers mostly drown out the weeds and what are weeds but wild plants we can't control, or "misplaced plants," as the adage goes.

I don't go out to hose Comet until it's nearly noon. It's a perfect summer day, not a cloud in the sky, the temperature already nearing 30 degrees Celsius. I know there's lots I should be doing, not the least of which is writing, and so I feel a twinge of guilt as I haul out my riding boots from the basement. I make smoked Gouda and spinach sandwiches, and take a few bottles of cider from the fridge. When Emilie pulls into the yard with her horse trailer, any doubts I've had about frittering away my day on a horse ride have vanished. One thing I know for sure is that there has never been a moment wasted in Emilie's company.

With our lunch, my hat and my gloves, I hop into Emilie's truck. We drive a few miles north on the Rolla Road to the Peace View Cemetery. Like most of the cemeteries in this country, this one, set on the bank of the Kiskatinaw River, has an excellent view. Northeast past the rolling hills and the bleached clay cliffs, you can see where the river flows into the Peace. The Kiskatinaw is the river I love; it's the one I grew up by. On the one hand I love seeing the river, but on the other hand I dread the nostalgia and feeling of loss that brings. I know by heart the dirt trails to the river, the swimming holes and, as summer wears on and the water becomes shallow and clear, where to wade for ammonites, their fluted shapes catching my eye. I know the bend in the river where the geology changes and the fossils become more clam-like and where a hill glitters with gypsum. My father had shown me all those places as a child, and then, when their turn came, he showed my children.

There is an old metal archway you have to pass beneath to reach the Peace View Cemetery, the archway painted white, the name in raised metal letters, and on the back of the arch, the words GOD BLESS YOU, rusted and faded but still blinding in the glare of the afternoon sun. We park on a grassy knoll and unload the horses, cracking open a cider as we put on our horses' saddles and bridles. We ride down the road until we come to a small opening in the trees and go through it, finding ourselves on an ATV trail that winds through poplars lush with leaves—a trail that gently descends to the river.

I remain a self-conscious rider. I ride as though I am being watched. And most of the time I am. Emilie analyzes whether I'm sitting the horse, or sitting on the horse, whether or not my feet are properly set in the stirrups. Do I look at ease? Like me, the horses know Emilie is their leader.

The riders who go into the mountains with Wayne include plenty of skilled horse people, but there are also those who have never ridden before. The horses are accustomed to that and the riders learn that they need only to be balanced and alert and the horses will take them where they need to go. Emilie likes to say that the horses on Wayne's pack string carry people like baggage. When I ride with Emilie I try not to be baggage, so every now and then I get Sally to trot up beside Emilie, and a few times we pass her and take the lead. I can do it, but it's work. When we reach the river we stop to eat our lunch along the bank. Watching the brown water rush by, I realize again how much I miss its silty current, the sheer clay banks, the swallows nesting beneath the cliff's overhang. But the rocks along the shore on this part of the river are different from those where I grew up. Here the rocks are not fossil-like. They are just regular stones.

"Sally likes you," Emilie says, as she always does, but today she seems more adamant. All through the day she says, "I think you need to buy Sally." And all through the day I consider her offer. I've been thinking that Comet could use a friend, a horse that's not likely to push him around. Bailey is too spirited and Ronnie, another gelding, would stir Comet up. Back home on the deck, emboldened by the day's ride and a glass of wine, we seal the deal. I write Emilie a cheque. Emilie takes it, and we clink our glasses. When Emilie drives out of the yard, Sally is left behind in a pen next to Comet.

I have bought myself a horse, something I would never have imagined myself doing, and not just in my old life, but also in my new. What have I done?

Wayne and I are on top of the world in the Southern Caribou Range.

TWENTY-FOUR

Hooping the Badlands

Each year, when Wayne returns home from the summer's expeditions, there is a resettling period that is as awkward as it is exciting. Sometimes we go away to disconnect from where we've each spent our summers. One year, we went on a short holiday to the central Alberta badlands. It was the year I'd taken up hula-hooping, something I'd done as a child, but had forgotten about until that summer, when a young woman at the Rolla Pub showed me a hula-hooping trick and I was so inspired I bought the thing from her—PVC tubing wrapped in black-and-red surveyor's tape. I hooped afternoons in Emilie's studio, narrowly missing her sculptures while she laughed and budgies flew in circles above our heads. I hooped after work, friends urging me on from the wooden deck—warm August nights on the lawn, northern lights huffing away; by the big weeping birch in the rain.

By September I could swing the hoop up past my chest, to my neck, a few lumbering loops around the throat before lifting it into the air, spinning it loose in my hand, then bringing it back down. On the eve of our road trip, I hooped toward the Oldsmobile and shoved it in.

We drove under a gentian blue sky, a blue that dissolved to a paleness at the horizon, the sky so broad and uninterrupted I swear its curvature showed, giving me a glimpse of more than a dome as it rounded the distant edges of the wheat fields now being swathed into blond, pillowy lines.

"I watched a YouTube," I told Wayne, "where someone stuck a camera to a hula hoop so it faced inward, toward the person, and when you watched it, it was like the person was spinning but the hoop was still. It was amazing."

"You were seeing it from the perspective of the hula hoop," Wayne said, "which is not your usual point of view." He looked pleased, as though he'd explained everything. *Good point,* I thought. Sometimes my point of view is that I stay in Rolla expediting guests in and out of the mountains, keeping the books and the yard together, going to work while Wayne travels up and down one mountain pass after another. My perspective is that it's easier for Wayne. He's having more fun. My perspective is that the experiences I've had pale in comparison to his. Although I imagine his own frame of reference would go something like this: this is how to raise awareness of the Muskwa–Kechika. He leaves our yard in June and returns in September. The trail is rigorous and the days are long.

A road sign told us we were getting close to the park. The late-day autumn light cut deep shadows into the earth, lifting the swaths of grain into relief, the combines' chaff furring the air a sweet amber and every now and then a slough flashed by, the water sucking in the shadows, the ponds dark and gleaming, ducks glinting on top, and above us the moon had begun to show, a salt tablet gaining in brightness until it stung my eyes as we crossed a landscape that never stopped, then did, all at once.

We'd arrived at a mesa-like brink, its edge dropping five hundred feet into a broad valley. Miles of prairie slammed to a stop.

"Whoa!" I said. "I did not see that coming." The scene stopped my breath. It was as if the past had been made transparent.

"It looks so puny," I said, looking down at the Red Deer River. It's hard to imagine that the river has cut down through the sediments, year after year, carrying the soil away, opening up this canyon, how the perpetual movement of wind and water has sculpted the earth, scoured through clay and sandstone to form hoodoos—pillars of sediment with a resistant rock on each top like an umbrella. The shape of the valley's humps and hillocks, heavy with clay, looked organic—soil rising into muscled shoulders, elephantine legs. The clay, cracked from the dry microclimate of the valley, has the texture of leathery hide, the hills ribboned with layer upon layer of sediment, like rings around a bathtub.

"Each era," I said softly, drawing in my breath, "sucked down the drain."

The place seemed to have stopped, as though it were under a spell. I knew it wasn't true. The forces of wind and water were still at work, I just couldn't see it.

We drove down the steep and winding clay road to the river, the watercourse looking a little more substantial close up, and parked along its bank at the picnicking site. A sign told us the bentonite in the clay could become slippery and impassable when wet, and we could not stay the night. The only sound was the wind, slewing the aspen leaves that had fallen to the ground. *I am a part of this*, I thought. *I am also apart.*

Wayne opened the trunk of the car and took out his backpack. I saw my hula hoop.

"What the hell," I said.

I hoisted the hoop over my shoulder and we struck off through scrub brush and grass meadow. The sun was at the horizon now, a waxen pool of red and orange, the heat of the day still cupped in the valley, the air pungent with dust and sage. A deer on the rise of a hill thrashed the brittle leaves of a willow with his antlers, antlers that had grown through the summer faster than snap beans. I've read that touching the branches of the willows with the tips of their tines, the palms of their racks, helps the animals rub off their velvet, but Wayne thinks it also helps them to know what they've become. The buck, tawny as the muted landscape, saw us too. He lifted his head, muscles tight, ears and tail flicking. He stared. We stared.

We reached the sand flats, and then scrambled up a clay bluff. I grabbed one of the rocks for balance and it was warm, the sun's rays drawn in, now radiating out. We reached the top of the hill to another panorama of striated earth.

Wayne bent down and picked up a chalk-coloured rock with a pink glaze. He handed it to me. "A dinosaur bone," he said. I touched my tongue to the object's cool surface. The rock stuck, locking my tongue to its papery grip. A paleontologist had shown Wayne this diagnostic trick—and Wayne had shown it to me—but, so focused on finding bone, he hadn't asked how it worked. I turned the fossil over in my hand.

"Probably a piece of hadrosaur rib," Wayne said.

A duck-billed dinosaur, the hadrosaur was one of the most common dinosaurs in the badlands. "Cows of the Cretaceous," Wayne likes to say. Like cows, hadrosaurs ate grass and moved in herds. Unlike cows, they laid eggs and were each roughly the size of an elephant. The dinosaur whose bone I'm holding lived sixty-seven million years ago. Who knows how it died, but a bone bed, like many found in the badlands, suggests a major event. Maybe mass starvation. Maybe a flood that swept the dinosaurs downstream as they tried to cross a swollen river, the swirling eddies and whirlpools sucking the animals to the bottom where the water's current moved them around until silt covered them, preserved them. As their bodies decomposed, the minerals in the surrounding sediments would have replaced the dinosaur's bones molecule by molecule, turning them from organic to mineral, sometimes with such fidelity that even the structure of the cells were retained.

"Maybe," said Wayne, "the molecules of dinosaur bones have the same structure as Velcro. That's why they stick to our tongue."

Wayne headed toward another cliff, his agile body moving easily over sandstone and boulders.

I set the rib down. Dry Island Buffalo Jump is a provincial park and you can't take fossils with you. And why would you want to? If I had taken the dinosaur bone home, it would have sat on the sill of my window. And then what? A moment, *this moment*, can't be kept. Standing there, the past pried open, made my life feel not just short, but petty. The time in which my worries would matter were clearly far less than the time in which they wouldn't. I found this strangely comforting, and then astonishing, that I was standing here at all, knowing I was not yet a part of the past. And my capacity to apprehend my amazement struck me as something special, almost omnipotent. I felt a flush of excitement, as if I were on to something. And then it was gone.

I put the hoop around my waist, positioning it so it pressed into my back. I felt its shape and weight before giving it a spin. It circled my body like a moon's orbit, the plastic tubing revolving so fast that static electricity raised the hairs on my arms; around me the hills, their bands of strata like tracings of the Earth's rotation.

I spun the hoop and took the moment in: here were my bones and here were the bones of creatures who lived millions of years before me. Here were my feet planted on the same soil dinosaurs roamed. And here was Wayne, returned, his bones asserting themselves as they always had.

I smiled and put down the hoop. He walked over. I placed my hands on the blades of his shoulders. Wayne has a laugh that is something like a chuckle but deeper, a low rich sound whose reverberations fill my body. He lifted me off the ground and twirled me, spinning until we blurred.

Sally (left) quickly becomes Comet's groupie. DONNA KANE

TWENTY-FIVE

Comet and Sally

After a few days of acquainting Sally with Comet, Comet with Sally, I put them together in Comet's pen. Almost instantly, she's fawning. I'm glad they've clicked, it's what I'd hoped for, and the fact that Comet has the upper hand was actually necessary to my plan, but I can't help feeling just a little annoyed by Sally's submissiveness. I think again of what Wayne says about horses being a reflection of the human who owns them. Sally doesn't seem to mind that Comet is the boss; she follows Comet around regardless of how much attention he pays her.

I learn that Comet has a jealous streak. If I brush Sally, Comet wants to be brushed too. When I pitch hay, Comet chases Sally off, and only when I've pitched enough hay for both does Sally return. Because of this, I've been taking Sally out of the corrals, tying her up to the hitching post in front of the tack shed to brush her, leading her around the yard out of sight of Comet. Which makes her nervous. The house makes her nervous, the trees by the dugout make her nervous. The flowerbeds make her nervous.

One afternoon I saddle Sally and ride her around in the corral. It goes well, but I can tell by Sally's ears, by her halting movements, that she's guessing at what I want. I can see I'm not making myself clear. And I know I'm not making myself clear, because I don't even know what it is that I want. I'm still trying to figure out what I want to do. My friend Joyce says to take baby steps, to take it slow, that the important thing is for both of us to feel comfortable. Emilie is waiting for me to ride Sally across the fields to her house.

The entire summer has been a blur. A few weeks ago we had a thunderstorm that shook the house. Four weeks ago I went to see my kids. Once, while visiting my parents, I tried to wake my father from a nap and couldn't. I called 911. The ambulance came. "He's having a stroke," they said.

"No heroics," I told them, and I know there was a kind of hysteria in my voice. I said it more than once—"Whatever you do, no resuscitation." The thought of him paralyzed and spending the rest of his years in a comatose state terrified me. I know he probably didn't mean it when he asked me to put him out of his misery if he ever got the way he's become, and that even if he did mean it, he's no longer the person who once made me promise. But there's a part of me that thinks, *If this is the end, how lucky.* It would mean he was going without visible pain; it would mean he'd never have to go into long-term care, something he'd always dreaded. But he does come out of it. At the hospital, in Emergency, his eyes start to flutter and then open. "I'll bet you thought I was dead," he says.

The next time Wayne phones I tell him I can't come to Mayfield. "I can't leave my mom. And I would never forgive myself if my father dies and I'm not here." There is a long pause before Wayne responds. "Well," he says, "you have to do what you have to do."

"To thine own self be true," Wayne will say, and what he means is, if you're not happy doing something, then don't do it. I knew Wayne would be disappointed that I wasn't coming in this year. I also knew that if I went through huge machinations to make it work, he'd be happy—but only if I was. Just as he took seriously his own desires and dreams, he assumed that I would as well. It had taken me years to believe that. I was more used to the politeness strategy in which invitations were made as expected gestures, not to be taken seriously. When I first met Wayne, I made all kinds of offers, and Wayne's response was always, "That would be good." It had taken me aback, and feeling somehow duped, I'd honour the offer, but then feel bitter about it. "But you offered," Wayne would say when I'd fall apart over it. Now I know that what he really means is, I have to do what I have to do.

Some days, Comet's wound looks like a riverbed, all pebbly and log-jammed, the water coursing its way through. Other days it looks more like the bark of a cottonwood tree. His wound, as it heals, grows itchy. When I scratch the hide that edges the wound, Comet's lower lip drops and quivers with pleasure.

When a wound begins to heal, the undamaged hide gathers itself together and stitches inward, closing in on the wound like fine embroidery, creating at first a thin outside ring of white. So beautiful and precise, that bit of white, so neatly and tightly woven to the edge of the wound, like a moon's crescent of light and within the wound, the scabs now come off with hardly any bleeding. As I hose, I pull the loose skin off. I rub the wound with my hand to loosen little bits of straw and leaf. I press my hand against the wound. Something about the heat from his body transferring to mine is soothing. Maybe it's because I am touching something that was once so damaged. I am touching something that is nearly healed.

TWENTY-SIX

Leading Sally

Over the past few weeks I've been turning the garden shed into Sally's tack shed. Comet's too. I've bought my own halters for both of them, a caddy, my own brushes and oat dishes. I buy wooden letters that spell SALLY'S SHAK and nail them to the door. I've bought enough to say "and Comet's too," but I haven't had the nerve to put them up. I have been thinking about it, though, of telling Wayne that Comet's mine.

The other day Emilie drove over and I put a halter on Sally and we walked her back to Emilie's. We did this so that Sally and I could get used to the route. We travelled west across the road from my house, over the golden stubble of a harvested wheat field, then into the next quarter of land where swaths of canola were drying—we walked along the edge so we wouldn't damage the crop. We walked over clods of dirt that had been worked up in the spring but not seeded, along a windbreak of poplars and pine trees, then through the brush and out into another field, then across the Rolla Road where vehicles roared along, then into the next quarter section with its swaths of wheat. The whole time Emilie was instructing me on how to lead Sally.

"You need to walk right beside her head," she'd say. "Don't let her get ahead of you." On the trail, the horses know to follow behind. Sally seemed only to want to be ahead of me, and I was constantly trying to stop her, turning her in a circle, and then starting again, the day hot as we continued through the field where we negotiated over and between swaths of grain. To my left I could see the pub and the store, the houses of Rolla and beyond them, to the west, Sweetwater Road and in its distance, Emilie's ranch. At one point, tired of listening to Emilie's constant instructions and Sally's refusal to comply, I flung the lead rope at Emilie and told her to do it herself. It wasn't my finest moment.

After I'd calmed myself down, apologized, taken Sally back, Emilie swatting me on the shoulder and laughing, we carried on, but this time Emilie held back. And I slowed down too. I'd been trying to keep up a pace that I thought would help me stay in sync with Sally. I thought Sally was comfortable with walking fast, and I wanted her to be comfortable. But it wasn't working. A resolve took hold. At the very least, I had to have a pace that was comfortable to me. And then, while I was focusing on that and trying to keep the speed consistent, Sally fell into line, slightly ahead of me, so that I was parallel to her shoulder. I let her.

And once that position was established, she kept to it. She didn't pull on the lead rope; she began to respond to the ebb and flow of my steps.

"You two look good together," Emilie said, joining us again. Then the three of us, together, walked the rest of the way to her ranch in sync, Sally on one side of me, Emilie on the other.

I watch as horses and riders cross a snowfield.

TWENTY-SEVEN

Season's End

Whether it is visible or not, a wound is what has been taken away, an absence made present by pain: a failed marriage, the loss of place, a gash to the flesh. As Comet's wound disappears, he needs me less and less. Healing, it seems, creates its own kind of absence. It is late summer now, the flowers have started to ripen off, the saskatoons along the driveway have shrivelled up, the pods of the caragana are popping, clicking in the late summer heat like a cooling engine. The geese are gathering with their lustrous honking. The cluster of gnats that peppered the air by Sally's shed all summer long—giving the air muscle and flex, a frivolity to their cloud of barely there, an air of we're just hanging out, busy at nothing, beach bums of the prairie—have disappeared.

The weather these past few weeks has been spectacular. The temperature hot, the yellow stubble of the harvested crops against the blue sky a confection of fulfillment. Today I rode Sally to Emilie's. I led her across the road that goes past our house into the first field, then the second and through the break in the bush that leads to the field before the highway. Once across the highway, I got on. And we rode, just me and Sally. Maybe not completely calmly: for sure there was a simmering excitement in me that I was doing this thing on my own, on a horse far from Wayne's lead or Emilie's, and Sally seemed to need my reassurance, her ears swivelling to my words. But as we rode along— my mind always on the next few feet; glancing, when I felt confident, at Emilie's ranch in the distance; feeling Sally's muscles as they moved—we were calm enough. When we rode into Emilie's driveway, I tied Sally up to the hitching post. And then, after I'd had some time to take it all in, Emilie and I rode back. After she left, I walked around the yard, the air still warm but dusk coming on. I carried a glass of wine and I looked at the flowers, at Sally's shed, at the apple trees and the lilac trees. I sat on the fence and I watched Comet and Sally. I was tired, but I was happy.

Parts of Comet's wound have closed altogether and the parts still open are only a few inches wide. I still hose him, but not every day. When I do, I know it is as much for me as it is for Comet. I also know that the pleasure I gain from this time together, from seeing the changes in the wound, rubbing away bits of straw or dead skin, is a pleasure beyond my affection for the horse. It has something to do with seeing things through. I am proud of the way Comet's healed.

After seven years of being a part-time rider on the trail, after a summer of hosing Comet, I have become more relaxed. I know that I am beginning to trust my ability to communicate with a horse and to let the horse communicate with me. But there's something else too. At the end of it all, there still isn't anything I really want from a horse. There is nothing I really want a horse to do.

"I disagree," Emilie says. "I think you're being too hard on yourself."

But here's the thing: When I'm out in the pasture, I'm keyed on the horses. But when I'm elsewhere, I still think about that Italian bicycle and the Vancouver seawall.

Riders lead their horses up Steeple Pass.

TWENTY-EIGHT

Tying Off

A knot is a line looped into itself until it binds, a topological solution to a fastening problem. As a mathematical construct, knots possess elegance and clarity. They are an example of the human intellect at work. Most knots used today have been used for thousands of years, and that is one of the reasons Wayne loves them, for their visceral connection to history—and for the way they do their job, and, when you get good at it, for the pleasure of loop and lock.

On the trail, the diamond hitch is the knot that holds the panniers and soft packs on the back of the horse. It's an art, and outfitters will eye each other's knots as a way of assessing worth. Part of what I love about the diamond hitch is that it is not just Wayne's fingers that move—his whole body is engaged in a union with the rope, a dance of tug and twist, the horse the object of the knot's enclosure.

Knots are anything but wild. If knots are tied correctly, they have the last word. They stop things and they hold them fast. Some people welcome answers that can contain their panicked moments. It keeps them from losing their minds. Others lose their minds because their ideas get all knotted up—a knot encloses a hole. Is the hole something or is it nothing? If it's nothing, is that not still something? Some of us drive ourselves crazy because we want the perfect answer to our problems.

Novelist Edith Wharton famously wrote, "I wonder, among all the tangles of this mortal coil, which one contains tighter knots to undo, and consequently suggests more tugging, and pain, and diversified elements of misery, than the marriage tie." We tie the knot and then we try to untie it.

When the last pack horse is packed, and Wayne is nimbly braiding the daisy-chained tail, it is the signal that the day has begun. Waiting for that last pack horse, for that final daisy chain to bind is both spectator sport and stopwatch. By the time that last slip knot is spent, you'd better be up on your horse and ready to go.

"Knots are real," Wayne will say. "They keep a person honest." If a knot is incorrectly tied, you'll know it. The horse will break free of its tree during lunch, the packs will shift on the downhill slope, the hobble will come off in the night.

Thinking about knots reminds me of Plato and trying to work my way through the "Form" of the forms. The idea being that for every object on Earth, there is a concept of that object. A horse is a form of Beauty. Beauty is the Form of the horse. And the Form of the Form? The idea of the idea? I felt trapped inside my skull, a physical discomfort from trying to wrestle my way out of logic. Aporia. To be stunned. To have nothing to hang on to. In *Plato as Artist*, philosopher poet Jan Zwicky writes, "Thinking leads to skepticism: that is its only defensible result. But it is not an acceptable result—not only can it precipitate cynicism and its attendant lassitudes, it cripples thinking itself." And that's not good. I need to think. If I don't, if my thoughts can't move, I might as well be dead. "The aim, then," Zwicky writes, "must be to contain thinking, while keeping it alive. And—Plato's insight—it turns out that life-sustaining thinking is impossible without hope."

We are trapped inside our skulls, limited by our own particular way of thinking. But within that space we make room for hope. Hope, Zwicky suggests, is the oxygen that gives thought breath. But unlike recognizing the Form of Beauty, where we can look at a horse and say it is beautiful, pointing to a single material object and saying it is hope is a lot harder. Maybe hope is the material world all told. Maybe hope emerges from our apprehension of the natural world's persistent and enduring qualities. After all, what hope tells us is that it may not be over; there might be another way.

"All men by nature desire to know," Aristotle said. Humans love to think. When I do find a solution, when I learn something new, I feel something open while at the same time snug up inside me.

I love the physical pleasure of tying a knot too, and the knot I love most is the one used to tie off. More intricate than tying a lead rope to a tree, but unburdened by the strength required to hold a soft pack together, tying off is a sensuous pleasure. In practical terms, tying off holds the pack horses' headgear together—the halter, the nose basket and the hobble that is stored around the horse's neck during travel, all of the straps gathered and bound and enclosed by the lead rope so that the straps of the headgear are less likely to catch on a branch of a tree or on another horse's gear as the horses tussle for position or one tries to scratch an itch.

To do this, to tie off and collect the gear together, you must first toss the lead rope over the horse's head and then bring the end of the rope under its neck. Then, with your left hand, you shape the rope into a sideways U held against the horse's cheek, and with your right hand bending the belly of the rope into its own smaller U, you pass the U behind the rope of the hobble, the strap of the nose basket, the crown strap of the halter, pushing that U-ed rope behind every last strap and then pushing it through the larger U that's been waiting on the other side; then you repeat that, then snug everything up and, with what's left of your lead rope, make a half hitch and put the tail through.

There is no way I would be able to tie the knot on that description alone. I need to be able to see the rope, to feel it in my hand. My body remembers the motions of the knot better than my thoughts do. And my body learns knots best when I make up a story—the gopher goes through the hole, the fox chases its tail—a story made up of the material world. When my body takes over, the pleasure of the knot takes hold. And once the knot is tied, I want to tie another one.

Wayne surveys his pack string. SARAH HAGGERSTONE

TWENTY-NINE

Coming Home

The thing I love most about meeting Wayne at the end of each summer is how I do everything I did in the spring but in reverse. In retracing my steps, I feel like I'm tying things up. The lawn that has been mowed countless times in Wayne's absence has now turned brown. The weeping birch, which I watered all summer long, trying to keep it lush while the woodpeckers perforated its bark, is drawing in its sap, its leaves turning orange. The flowerbeds that were just getting started when Wayne left have flourished and grown; the leaders of the new spruce trees extend like articulated tent poles; the fleece flower having burst into bloom, now drops its seeds. It is like a door opened in the spring, and I entered it, and now, early fall, I have come back out. And Wayne is coming out too. This year, he will come out at the Tetsa River.

I know when I see him I'll make strange. On the one hand, it's exciting to discover his body anew, but on the other, I worry. What if we've both changed in ways we don't like? And I don't just mean in a carnal way, though I mean that too. What if we don't like each other in *any* way? And what about those female clients who spend so much time on the trail with him? There's a life-and-death quality to the experience. Crossing a river or leading a horse up a pass can be a life-changing experience, and when the group shares that experience, the bonding can be profound. I've mentioned this to Wayne, always careful to make it seem as though I'm teasing, nothing serious. It's a delicate line we draw. A part of him is likely reassured that I am concerned, though he never comes out and says that. What he does say, and what, at the end of the day, I believe to be true, is that there is no one else.

I park in the pullout, an hour ahead of his estimated time of arrival. I want to prepare for it, be ready for the moment when he emerges from the trees. But somehow, no matter how carefully I watch, he always surprises me, and this time too, appearing as if out of nowhere on Bonus, a firefly let loose from its jar. Because of the routine of the trail, even now, even after three months, Wayne and I barely have time for a hug. Along with the rest of the crew we set to unpacking the pack horses; and because we are now beside the highway, we have to tie them to the trees and feed them flakes of hay, just as we did on their way in.

I have so much to tell him. My news padded with the clicks and whirs of electricity and vehicles and news wire—I flew to Vancouver to visit my kids, Mavericks Night Club burned down, my dad had another stroke, BC Hydro's proposed dam has moved into the joint review stage. Wayne's news will be more focused, the world revolving around his pack string: they watched a grizzly chase two elk calves who deked the bear out in the willows; they glassed a stone sheep coming out of a set of cliffs, then another one, until they'd counted fifty. Michael Coon, who'd been on the trail twelve times, confessed he'd never been to the top of a mountain, so the next chance they got, they climbed one. And a turquoise down jacket, lost the season before, was found in perfect shape, in a patted-down patch of grass where bears had been playing.

Comet stands behind Sally's Shak.

THIRTY

Sally and Comet

Today I took down the temporary electric fencing I'd put up around the hay bales in the area where the granaries were and where Comet and Sally spent their summer. With Wayne home, we've moved Comet, Sally, Ronnie and Bailey into the front pasture, and I've been pitching hay there. I can see them now on the little hill where Brian and I, during the summer, would take Comet and Sally for walks around the pasture, then stop to let them eat the grass.

When I took the electric fencing away, it left a sharp boundary between the side where the horses came to eat, their hooves trampling the ground into pulverized dirt, and the hay side, where the grass was intact but now brown.

The pitchforks are still leaning against the bales, and it makes me strangely homesick. I realize how rich and full my summer has been, and how attached

I've become to taking care of Comet. I think of my dad, how he's still hanging on though it is getting steadily harder for my mom to care for him at home. This week, we put him on the list for long-term care. When I see him, he doesn't always know who I am. But I can tell, even if he doesn't know my name or what my relationship is to him, that I am familiar. His eyes still light up when he sees me.

When Wayne comes home, I try to make my claim. Comet is mine now. I've earned him. And he belongs to Sally too. But with the other horses home from the trail, grazing in the harvest field next door, Comet is spending much of his time leaning over the fence whinnying at them.

"Comet wants to be with the rest of the horses," Wayne keeps saying. Soon we will ride the other horses across the fields a few miles northeast of our place to a quarter section of pasture, where they will graze through the winter.

"Ronnie would be better for Sally," Wayne says. "He wouldn't boss her around the way Comet does."

Which, I have to admit, bothers me too. I feel my resolve start to wane. Also, I don't like the idea of Comet staying with Sally if what he wants is to be somewhere else. But if he does go with the other horses, he'll probably end up being a part of Wayne's herd and next year he'll be back on the trail.

"Okay," I say, finally. "Let's try it."

"Well then," Wayne says, "go get your horse."

Comet and Sally have moved from the hill back to the water bowls. I walk up to Comet and stand beside him. I touch his scar. I press the palm of my hand against him. I could stand and touch his scar all day. I put his halter on and lead him to the fence that separates him from the rest of the herd. I take off his halter and open the gate. He gallops toward the other horses, and they gallop to meet him and then they all run together across the field. Comet is almost lost in the herd, but I can still see his mane, the colour of stubble flashing in the sun.

Sally is beside herself, frantic and whinnying, running up and down the fenceline.

"She'll be all right," Wayne says.

And perhaps she would have been. But it was Comet who, after a few hours, left the other horses and came back to the fence. After a few days with Comet still choosing to graze near the fence that separated him and Sally, Wayne let him back in. At least for the winter he'll stay with Sally. In the spring, we will see.

Horses survey the Southern Caribou Range.

The Wild

Who can know the mind of another being? Who can even know their own? I watch the horses. There is a power and a grace we recognize as beauty, a beauty we want to be a part of. And if that means thousands of years of human intervention, of domestication, to capture even a small part of that beauty, we do it. And the horses let us.

I watch Wayne. There are aspects of him I'll never understand. One is how he stays so optimistic about places like the Muskwa–Kechika, how he continues to believe that wilderness areas can be kept from human industry. But then again, it is Wayne who says you can't be an environmentalist unless you are an optimist. The way Wayne thinks is a mystery to me. It's one of the things I love about him.

I watch my dad. It seems that what's disappearing is his consciousness, as if his body can no longer absorb it. Maybe awareness is leaving my dad's corral, returning to the cosmic plain from which it came. There is so much about our brain, our bodies, our minds we still don't understand.

There are things I never thought I could do, but I did them. At first, the shock of it felt impossible to overcome, but then, the realization that I'd survived built a new and more solid foundation inside me, a foundation that gave rise to infinite possibilities, an endless rolling out of *What next?* And *Why not?*

Like other beings, the natural world keeps me alive, both physically and metaphysically. The Muskwa–Kechika is a place that still feels pristine, exuberant, healthy, still filled with its original potential, its infinite possibilities, its mysteries. When I am there, it restores me. I breathe better. It fuels my curiosity, my desire to always be thinking and in that thinking, to experience the wild. I hope it can stay that way.

A horse in the wild.

Bibliography

Aristotle. *Aristotle: Selections.* Translated by Terence Irwin and Gail Fine. Indianapolis, IN: Hackett Publishing Company, 1995.

Armitage, Simon. *Walking Home.* New York: W.W. Norton and Company, 2012.

Cahn, Steven M., et al. *Knowledge and Reality: Classic and Contemporary Readings.* Upper Saddle River, NJ: Pearson Education, 2004.

Critchley, Victoria. "Protecting the 'Serengeti of the North': The Campaign for the Muskwa–Kechika." *Environmental Campaigns: Strategies & Tactics.* Ed. Michael Northrop. Yale University: School of Forestry and Environmental Studies 847b, Spring 05.

Davis, Wade. *The Wayfinders.* Toronto: House of Anansi Press, 2009.

Diamond, Jared. *Guns, Germs, and Steel.* New York: W.W. Norton and Company, 1997.

Hunt, Ray. Website at http://www.rayhunt.com. Accessed on August 5, 2017.

Joyce, James. *A Portrait of the Artist as a Young Man.* London: Penguin Books, 1972.

Leopold, Aldo. *A Sand County Almanac.* New York: Ballantine Books, 1977.

Lilburn, Tim. *Living in the World as If It Were Home: Essays.* Dunvegan, AB: Cormorant Books, 1999.

Marshall, Robert. "The Problem of the Wilderness." In *The Scientific Monthly* vol. 30, No. 2 (Feb., 1930), pp. 141–148. Accessed at http://www.jstor.org/stable/pdf/14646.pdf?seq=1#page_scan_tab_contents on August 5, 2017.

McCaslin, Susan. "Facing the Environmental Crisis with Contemplative Attention: The Ecopoetics of Don McKay, Tim Lilburn, and Russell Thornton." In *Research Review: A Special Topics Journal from the University of the Fraser Valley,* vol. 3 issue 1 (Winter 2010): 64–82.

McKay, Don. *Deactivated West 100.* Kentville, NS: Gaspereau Press, 2005.

———. *Vis à Vis: Field Notes on Poetry and Wilderness.* Kentville, NS: Gaspereau Press, 2001.

Merleau-Ponty, Maurice. *Phenomenology of Perception.* London and New York: Routledge, 2002.

———. *The World of Perception.* London and New York: Routledge, 2002.

———. *The Primacy of Perception.* Northwestern University Press, 1964.

Muskwa–Kechika Advisory Board. "Muskwa–Kechika Management Area." Accessed at http://www.muskwa-kechika.com on July 16, 2017.

Plato. *Republic.* Translated by G.M.A. Grube. Revised by C.D.C. Reeve. Indianapolis, IN: Hackett Publishing Company, 1992.

Remuda Horsemanship Program. Home page accessed at https://www.facebook.com/Remuda Horsemanship on July 16, 2017.

———. "Remuda Program: Part 1." Accessed at http://www.youtube.com/watch?v=nvTJQ8481_Y on July 16, 2017.

Rilke, Rainer Maria. *Duino Elegies,* 4th ed. Translation, introduction and commentary by J.B. Leishman and Stephen Spender. London: Chatto and Windus, 1975.

Sawchuk, Wayne. "Muskwa–Kechika: A Pictorial History." *Living Landscapes: Royal BC Museum.* Accessed at https://royalbcmuseum.bc.ca/exhibits/living-landscapes/prnr/muskawa_kechika_histrical/index.html on August 3, 2017.

———. *Muskwa–Kechika: The Wild Heart of Canada's Northern Rockies.* Dawson Creek, BC: Peace Photographics, 2004.

———. "Wayne Sawchuk's Muskwa–Kechika." Accessed at http://www.muskwa-kechika.com on July 16, 2017.

Smith, George. "Birth of a Campaign." Accessed at http://cpaws.org/about/cfy-story-george-smith-2 on July 16, 2017.

Thomas, Nigel J.T. "Mental Imagery." In *The Stanford Encyclopedia of Philosophy* (Spring 2017), edited by Edward N. Zalta. Accessed at https://plato.stanford.edu/archives/spr2017/entries/mental-imagery/ on July 16, 2017.

Zwicky, Jan. *Plato as Artist*. Kentville, NS: Gaspereau Press, 2009.

Acknowledgments

Sincere thanks to—

Lynne Van Luven, Katherin Edwards, Luanne Armstrong, Merilyn Simonds and Wayne Grady for weighing in on earlier versions of this manuscript. Barbara Berson for the touch of a jeweller's cloth, removing buildup and tarnish, helping to give my words a bit more lustre and finish; Cheryl Cohen, for the touch of a jeweller's loupe, catching and correcting details I would surely have otherwise missed.

Anna Comfort O'Keeffe for her friendly professionalism and all the folks at Harbour Publishing who guided me through the process with such expertise and good cheer.

Wayne, my family and my friends—thanks for being such fine company on this trail.

"The Gaze" was shortlisted for the Edna Staebler Personal Essay Contest and published in *TNQ*'s Summer 2016 issue.

Some lines in the book have been borrowed from previous poems of mine—"Absorption I" and "Absorption II," published in the Spring 2012 issue of *The Fiddlehead,* and "You Know Me Better than I Know Myself," published in *Erratic* (Hagios Press, 2007).